TRUE GHOST STORIES

HARRY LUDLAM

foulsham
LONDON • NEW YORK • TORONTO • SYDNEY

foulsham
The Publishing House, Bennetts Close,
Cippenham, Slough, Berks, SL1 5AP, England

ISBN 0-572-02543-2

Copyright © 2000 Harry Ludlam

All rights reserved.

The Copyright Act prohibits (subject to certain very limited exceptions) the making of copies of any copyright work or of a substantial part of such a work, including the making of copies by photocopying or similar process. Written permission to make a copy or copies must therefore normally be obtained from the publisher in advance. It is advisable to consult the publisher if in any doubt as to the legality of any copying which is to be undertaken.

Printed in Great Britain by St Edmundsbury Press, Bury St Edmunds, Suffolk.

Contents

The Beautiful Duchess	7
The Black Prince Rides	11
A Cottage in the Country	15
Calling in the Clergy	23
The Creep of Camberwell	33
Ghosts All His Life	43
Terror on Holiday	49
A Ghost at the Bank	53
The Town of Eight Hundred Ghosts	65
Strange Sounds of War	71
And They Came Back	77
The Mystic Healing Hand	85
The Mermaid of the Mere	91
What Price a Ghost?	101
The Hero of Jutland	107
Canon to the Rescue	113
The Trouble with Amy	119
Spirits at the Inn	129
Haunted to the Gallows	139
Diana's Grandfather	143
Living with a Ghost	147
The Head of Roger	157
Phantoms of the Roads	163
Margaret and Joe	167
Goosed by a Ghost	173
Join My Ghost Walk	179
She Walks the Castle	185
Ghosts 2000	189

By the same author:

A Biography of Dracula

The Mummy of Birchen Bower

The Restless Ghosts of Ladye Place

Elliott O'Donnell's Casebook of Ghosts

Elliott O'Donnell's Ghost Hunters

Ghosts Among Us

The fascination of ghosts, the real life kind, lies in the remarkable variety of forms that hauntings can take, and their stunning impact on those people fortunate – or unfortunate – enough to encounter them.

Real ghosts obey no natural laws. They are ageless, timeless. They emerge both in the dark and the daylight, and they appear mostly to ordinary people going about their everyday lives, people who have rarely given a second's thought to talk of ghosts.

But ghosts there are. A bewildering multiplicity of them.

Some hauntings I investigated have featured a single ghost, others several. Some had a handful of witnesses, others dozens. Some terrorised whole families, driving them out of their homes.

There are ghosts that appear fleetingly, others that linger for weeks or months, and some that persist for years. In my experience, a good number of these wandering earth-bound spirits are soon identified, but others remain a mystery until long afterwards.

There is absolutely nothing at all to compare with the spine-tingling sensation of seeing a ghost, or in making the chilling discovery that 'something' has invaded one's home. The shock. The wonderment. And, all too often, the distress. For some of the more troublesome ghosts can be noisy, cantankerous or of a decidedly evil nature.

My collection of true cases, drawn from all quarters of the ghost world, show how its restless spirits impinge on our lives. Every day. Everywhere. And how police, clergy and psychic investigators are called to the aid of those victims of hauntings reduced to desperate states.

My thanks to everyone for helping me to tell of these uncanny experiences just as they happened.

Harry Ludlam

The Beautiful Duchess

She was beautiful and sexy. She was without conscience, shame or fear. She was ambitious, extravagant, greedy, arrogant, vain, and possessed of a scandalous tongue. She was Elizabeth, Countess of Dysart, afterwards Duchess of Lauderdale, and she haunts Ham House, a mansion on the banks of the River Thames in Richmond, Surrey.

Elizabeth was the eldest daughter of the Earl of Dysart. Her parents having no son, a Royal charter was obtained to enable her to succeed to the title. In 1647 she married a baronet, Sir Lionel Tollemarche, and four years later they acquired Ham House, which had been built some forty years earlier.

Elizabeth was, as they say, the kind of girl who had been around, and they had not been married long before she became steeped in affairs, courtiers and dashing gallants flocking around her wherever she went. In earlier years she had had an affair with Oliver Cromwell, and now, with him gone and Charles II on the throne, her carryings-on with John Maitland, Duke of Lauderdale, were too much even for the court of the Merry Monarch. Through all this her husband, Sir Lionel, kept a low profile; bowing, it seems, to power and money.

The Countess's friendship with the Duke of Lauderdale dated back to pre-marriage days. She always maintained that she had only saved Lauderdale, a Royalist, from the scaffold by submitting to the desires of the Protector. But now, in the midst of their hot-blooded affair, she and Lauderdale quarrelled, for whatever reason, and a certain coolness arose between them. No matter, she was still intent on getting her man. When her husband, Sir Lionel, conveniently died, she at once made new advances to the Duke, with the result that his wife left him and went to live in Paris. She died three years later – and the way was clear for the Countess to become a Duchess. She finally landed Lauderdale in his fifties and they were married in 1671.

From the start of this new marriage it was the Duchess who ruled at Ham House, as she had done before. The Duke might be one of the King's more powerful ministers and a member of the secret council, the Cabal, but it was Elizabeth who wielded power at home. She saw to it that they lived in the grand manner, trying to outdo royalty in the splendour of their wild parties and other entertainments. Her jewellery and costumes were said to eclipse in cost and magnificence those of any other lady of the court. She filled the mansion with beautiful things: furniture, tapestries, draperies, pictures. She was a great survivor, remaining blithely untouched by the intrigues and dark deeds that went on around her in those days, and she also outlived her husband by many years. Lauderdale died in his sixties, in 1682; she lived on till 1698. She was succeeded in her estates and title of Dysart by her eldest son by her first husband, Lionel Tollemarche, the house remaining occupied by that family for the next two-and-a-half centuries.

And by the infamous old Duchess of Lauderdale herself, too. In the still hours of the night the tapping of heels and of a stick were sometimes heard crossing the polished oak boards of various of the rooms and ascending and descending the great staircase. Sometimes they stopped outside one room and sometimes another, and occasionally, not content with hovering outside, the Duchess's ghost would enter a room.

Late in the nineteenth century the haunting took a surprise turn. The little daughter of a butler at Ham House was on a visit to her father, by permission of the Tollemarche family, when she was awakened in the early hours of the morning by a curious noise in the room. Thinking it was either a mouse or a bird, she sat up and, looking in the direction of the sounds, saw a little old woman kneeling by the fireplace, scratching on the panelling of the wall with long, claw-like fingernails. Turning round and seeing the child gazing at her, the old woman got up and, leaning on the rail of the child's bed, stared fixedly at her. Her eyes glittered and her expression was so menacing that the child screamed and hid under the bedclothes. Fortunately some of the household were near at hand and came running to the room, but the ghost had vanished.

On recovering from her fright the child described what she had seen. The Tollemarches, who were told about it the next day, had the panelling removed. Behind it, it is recorded, were found old documents whose contents left little doubt that Elizabeth, Countess of Dysart, had murdered her first husband, Sir Lionel Tollemarche, in order to marry her long-standing love, the Duke of Lauderdale. The ghost the little girl had seen was in all probability that of the murderess.

It might be thought that the haunting would now stop, but it did not. The Duchess's phantom footsteps continued their occasional nightly progression, even when Ham House passed to the National Trust in 1948. They went on and on. In 1995, when a new property manager for the Trust moved into Ham House with her husband and three children, they had only been in the house two weeks when she was obliged to call in a priest to bless the top flat where they resided. This, apparently, improved the unpleasant atmosphere there, but it did not put an end to the Ham

House haunting – doors slamming, footsteps walking up and down stairs, patches of cold air invading certain parts of the old Stuart mansion. Just when it is thought the ghost has gone, back it comes again.

The bad, bad Duchess of Lauderdale seems intent on walking on into her fourth century, though she does have company. This, apparently, is her husband, the Duke, who, when also wandering about, gives off a most unpleasant smell of sweet pipe tobacco.

The Black Prince Rides

John Burnell saw the ghostly rider once only, when he was a young man, but the shock of that night encounter has haunted him every day of his life since. Although he is now in his eighties, what he saw on that night long ago remains as vivid as if it were yesterday.

Young John, who lived with his parents at Erith, Kent, was working as a railway booking clerk at Bexley station. In those days (the 1930s) rail booking offices remained open until the early hours of the morning. John was on the last shift of the day, staying on duty till 1.30 a.m. Then it was out with his bicycle and off home. It was a dark but clear night and John was glad to be on his way, looking forward to supper and bed. His route back to Erith was through Bexley, past the Black Prince, a well-known public house in that district, up Gravel Hill, through Bexleyheath and then on to the last miles home. Gravel Hill, a made-up road but very, very steep, was the only blot on the horizon, proving a tiring climb, but the twenty-year-old had walked up it with his cycle many times on his homeward journeys.

This night, as he wearily approached the crossroads by the pub, prior to the base of Gravel Hill, suddenly it happened. A man in full armour riding a black horse came out *through* a wall on the right, passed across the road in front of him and vanished into a high brick wall on the other side. As the figure emerged from the wall it was bigger than an ordinary rider but quite solid. The moonlight shone on parts of the rider's armour, especially the knee armour. Then the rider became smaller again as he disappeared into the wall opposite.

John was horrified. Shaking with fear, he had to gather all the strength and courage he possessed to mount his cycle and pedal fast every inch of the way home, pushing desperately up the impossible Gravel Hill and racing on for miles past. He arrived home in such a traumatic state, soaked with perspiration, that a doctor had to be called.

John remained severely shaken for two months. He refused to pass the same spot at night again and when he returned to work, managed to get his shift altered so that it ended earlier in the day. Meanwhile, his worried father, shocked by his son's absolute terror, made enquiries locally and found that John had certainly not been 'seeing things', for there had been earlier sightings of the Black Prince.

The source of the hauntings appeared to be Hall Place, a six hundred-year-old mansion near Bexley, with which the Black Prince, England's charismatic fourteenth-century royal hero, had definite links. Hall Place stood beside the roadway along which thousands of pilgrims to Canterbury passed. It was from Hall Place that Edward, Prince of Wales, the 'Black Prince', so-called because of the dark armour he favoured, set out for France to join his father (Edward III) in fighting the French. At the Battle of Crécy in 1346, when his father's English army won a glorious victory despite being outnumbered three to one, he was in the thick of the fighting, although then only sixteen. Ten years later, still only in his twenties, the Black Prince commanded an English and Gascon army that routed the French at the Battle of Poitiers, capturing Jean le Bon, King of France.

The Black Prince stayed at Hall Place several times on his way to the wars in France, where he spent much of his life on campaigns. Tradition has it that when he wooed and won Joan, the 'Fair Maid of Kent', they spent their honeymoon at Hall Place. And on his death, at the early age of forty-six, his body rested at Hall Place for one night on its way to Canterbury for burial.

The Black Prince's tomb in Canterbury Cathedral has his effigy 'armed in steel for battle', according to his wishes, with pieces of armour and clothing displayed nearby; and it is in full armour that his ghost has been reported to appear, usually at dusk, and sometimes with the sound of music played on antique instruments.

Among the best recorded sightings of the warrior Prince are those made by Lady Limerick, when she was resident at Hall Place in the 1920s. Three times she saw the ghostly figure of the Prince, clad in armour and, as she described it, 'shrouded in light'. He only remained for a second or two and then disappeared. On one occasion she saw him standing by the fireplace in her small dining room. Unusually, that was in the daytime.

On two other occasions during the First World War, when Britain was in grave peril, Lady Limerick saw the ghost in the evening, once in the chapel and later in one of the corridors upstairs. She said she always associated the appearance of the spirit with some national danger.

Had the Black Prince survived just a year longer he would have succeeded his father as King of England. But whether this or any other factor of his colourful life has any bearing on his continued haunting of Hall Place and surrounds is anybody's guess.

And as far as John Burnell is concerned, that one terrifying sight of him was more than enough.

A Cottage in the Country

For many townsfolk the dream is of a picturesque cottage in the country. Some realise their dream. Mrs Madeleine Scott did, she found her ideal cottage, but what she did not bargain for was what came with it.

From the moment that Madeleine, a busy young north London wife, set out on her search for a country retreat there was a sense of the inevitable.

She had spent happy weekends in that part of East Sussex known as '1066 country', after the Norman invasion, and found it held a certain something for her. Every time she drove down from London, on getting halfway she would feel a real buzz go through her. It was as if she had had a past life there. A girlfriend who often accompanied her experienced much the same thing, a warm feeling of coming home. So it was that Madeleine began looking for a cottage of her own in the area.

The first time she saw the cottage she ultimately bought she was with her aunt, down for another weekend of cottage-hunting. Madeleine would walk into a place and find herself saying 'No' straight away. 'No, no, no…' Then they came to this particular property, the last of a row of attractive old terraced cottages in the village of Guestling, near Hastings. As they walked up the path with the estate agent, Madeleine said to her aunt before even looking in the front window, 'I'm going to buy this'.

Her aunt told her not to be silly, they hadn't looked inside yet and anyway they had another two properties to see. But Madeleine was adamant. 'Look,' she told the agent, 'it's sold, I'm going to buy it.' He was flabbergasted but, she says, she *knew*. It was just as if somebody had touched her on the shoulder and said, 'Take it'. She would have bought it blind. They walked in the front door, which was at the side, and she said, 'Yes, yes, fine, fine, this is it.' The bemused agent asked, 'Aren't you going to see upstairs?' She did so. It was smaller than she thought, as her aunt was quick to point out. But, no, Madeleine said, it was perfect. She had a precise figure in mind as to how much she would offer. It was much below the price suggested, and at which it was put up for auction in Maidstone, but Madeleine was firmly convinced that the lower amount she had decided was exactly what she would pay. And so it transpired on the day: the hammer came down on her bid and the cottage was hers.

It needed a fair bit of work doing to it and she found a good builder, one who became so attached to the property he was improving that he came to look upon it almost as his own. Everything would go ahead, putting in beams, a fitted kitchen and all the rest, including work outside. But there proved to be something strange from the start.

Hastings builder Ray Mann first thought there was something a bit odd when his tools kept going missing. After vainly searching around for them he would turn in desperation to doing a different job, hoping to find the tools later – which he did; puzzlingly, they reappeared just where he had originally left them. Then, from being a nuisance, the situation became serious. On leaving work for the day Ray always double-locked the back door, by which he entered. One morning as usual he produced his key, only to find the door mysteriously unlocked. It happened again, and again. By now he was very concerned, as the property was his responsibility in the owner's absence. He phoned Madeleine in London to tell her what had happened: he was hours behind schedule because his tools kept going missing and on three occasions the securely locked door had unaccountably been unlocked overnight. 'You have "something" here,' he reported, 'there is no other possible explanation.'

And that was the onset of it all. One weekend Madeleine went down to the cottage with a girlfriend who, as soon as she entered, felt there was 'someone' there. Her unease soon turned to fright. They were both in the back bedroom, where there was a little bedside lamp on the window ledge. Madeleine's companion had her handbag open. Suddenly the light bulb twisted itself from its socket and flew out of the lamp into the air and down into her handbag. She shot downstairs in a terrible state and would never visit the cottage again.

Madeleine next went down with her aunt. Auntie always took a pot of chopped lemon because she liked lemon tea, and she always left the pot on the tea tray in the kitchen. They were at the cottage for three days, and every morning when Auntie got up she found the pot had transported itself down to the middle of the kitchen floor. She was convinced that her niece had got up in the night and moved it out of devilment. Madeleine could not tell her the truth, that there was a ghost about, or Auntie would have thought she was out of her mind.

Meantime, while Ray the builder was finishing off his work, the gas central heating kept being tinkered with, the timers altered, by someone or something turning and twisting the dials, and lights were switching themselves on. Ray was worried because he did not want to be thought responsible.

During Madeleine's first week's stay at the cottage her two dogs, an Old English sheepdog and a little crossbreed, were distinctly uneasy. They slept at the top of the stairs, but one night flew down in a panic.

'Teddy (the sheepdog) was extremely agitated, clinging to me, shaking and looking all round. Somebody was definitely in the cottage that night because I felt them as well, I sensed it was a woman. She must have gone up to the dogs, especially Lucy in her basket, and frightened them both into flying down the stairs. As I was trying to calm them down I felt the ghost woman come into the lounge and sort of breathe in and out.'

Now began a whole catalogue of strange events. Let Madeleine describe them:

'The next time my aunt came down she was woken at three o'clock in the morning by two loud bangs on the partition wall between her bedroom and the bathroom. She was very startled, didn't know where she was. She tried to get back to sleep but at four o'clock it happened again. Bang! Bang!

'I had a vase of flowers taken off a bedside table and put in the middle of my bedroom floor. The same thing happened down in the lounge.

'There were four of us at the cottage one misty midwinter's day and we came back about five o'clock to find that all the lights were on in the cottage. We got out of the car, all looked at one another and said, "Who did that, who left them on?" But nobody had, we were very careful about lights, yet these lights had been turned on in the kitchen and the lounge.

'It got to the point when weird things were happening all the time. On Christmas Eve in the middle of the night somebody sat on the foot of the bed my side and the bed went right down. I thought at first it was one of the dogs, but they could not climb on the bed as they were both too old, and they were not allowed to anyway. It woke me up but not Chris, my husband. After about a minute the bed went back to normal.

'On Christmas night when we finished playing cards all the cards were put in their right order, but on coming down next morning we found the whole lot shuffled together and totally out of order. Chris couldn't believe it, he was so positive, he knew what he had done, but the cards had been shuffled and it took twenty minutes to put them back as they were the night before.

'That evening as my friend Susan went into the lounge she exclaimed, "I don't know what's happening, it's so cold!" I had the central heating on but it was definitely very, very cold in there like I'd never known it before – like ice – and with it was a very strong smell of orange essence. Just like oranges, really strong. I left the room, went back in again and it had got stronger. But when we all went in about ten minutes later the smell had gone. There was absolutely nothing "orangey" in the house that could have produced the smell.

'The cottage has a sensor light that will pick up a fox, anything, even a high wind, it is so sensitive. It was four o'clock in the morning when the front doorbell rang. Chris went downstairs but there was nobody there at all and the sensor light had not come on, although it would pick up anything. You really had to put your finger on the bell to ring it.

'Another time when I was alone in the cottage there were two heavy knocks on the door, again about four o'clock in the morning. I went down, but again the sensor light was not on. I tested the knocker, giving it two heavy knocks, and that was the sound I had heard.

'And then, the toilet paper. I tend to have one sheet down, it's something I do, I've got a thing about it. But one night when I went upstairs to the bathroom the toilet paper had been pulled right the way down to the floor then come up again and wrapped round the toilet roll, which was totally out of order.

'A friend staying with me woke up in the night and swore she heard somebody coming up the stairs but stopping before they got to the top. Worse happened to my friend Jackie Robson: she kept having the cover pulled off her bed. It happened so often, waking her up, that she just used to plead, "I'm very tired, you are going to have to leave because I can't hear you and I can't see you."

'One night I was woken by a man entering my bedroom and crossing to the window to look out. I sat up in bed, scared, and he walked out of the room. Next morning I said to Jackie, "We had a visitor last night." She said, "Yes, I know." She told me that the same man had walked past her bed to her window. I started describing the man I had seen and she finished it off; we had both seen exactly the same figure. He was a tall man with fair hair, about mid-forties, and had the appearance of a land worker of bygone times.'

And then came the strangest of all nights.

'I am a heavy sleeper, but this night I suddenly woke up, wide awake, about three o'clock in the morning, to find the whole of the bedroom covered with a strange mist. It was all around me, lovely and calm: I felt I was drifting with it. It had a shimmer about it, rather like you see the shimmer of light on the sea. I thought, "What is going on?" for I could see it with my real eye, not half asleep. Then I saw in a corner of the room a shaft of light which did not touch the floor. It ended about a foot above the floor and was some three feet high, a square shaft of light that lit up the entire room. I thought it must be the light from a street lamp outside, until I suddenly remembered there were not any street lamps. There was no way there could be any light in the bedroom – but there it was. As I looked at it, it was just like a big pulsating balloon, bright orange. It pulsated and glowed and it moved, and I was spellbound. Jackie was in the other bedroom and I was conscious I could break the spell by calling out to her, when everything should go back to normal, but I wanted to stay watching as long as I possibly could to see what would happen next. The orange glow kept pulsating, pulsating, and out of it came colours of the rainbow. It was so peaceful ... yellows and greens ... and getting bigger, and I lay there wondering "What's going to happen now?" Then suddenly I felt I had got as far as I could go and I cried out aloud, "Enough, please, enough." I was too scared to go on. Then came the strangest thing of all, for I felt somebody (or something) touch the centre of my forehead with their finger, at which I went into a deep sleep until eight o'clock in the morning. Had I stayed the course I think I would have seen something, because the glow was getting bigger and bigger, but I was much too frightened to go on. When I think about it now I wish that I had held fast and not given in.'

Still the disturbances went on. Many a night after going to bed Madeleine thought she heard somebody tinkering around in the kitchen. Sometimes there would be a tapping and a rapping, making it difficult to get to sleep, but one night there was an almighty crash and she gingerly got up and went down, expecting to find something had fallen, but nothing had: everything was untouched and in its place. Not so on other nights. The doormat at the back door was of the thick, rushy type and was never moved, at least not by Madeleine or her husband. But many a time they came down in the morning to find the heavy mat moved to the opposite side of the kitchen. Then there were the constant playful little things, like Chris finding a jar of marmalade plucked from a basket overnight and dumped in the middle of the kitchen floor.

One evening as Madeleine watched television there was one of those occult 'reconstruction' programmes on which someone was describing how he had twice seen a ghost. 'Twice,' Madeleine found herself saying, 'what a fuss to make. They should come round here!'

And so it went on, even to invisible hands messing about with clothes. Madeleine went to the airing cupboard, which she always kept extremely tidy, towels in one place, sheets in another, to find one of her skirts which she had carefully hung in the wardrobe crumpled up and pushed into the airing cupboard.

A few questions asked around locally established the fact that a woman who had had the cottage way, way back had been bedbound for a number of years in the main bedroom. Other than that there was no explanation for the haunting, though the old cottages had seen plenty of life in their time; the one next door to Madeleine's, for instance, had once been used as a little pub, while another had been the village sweetshop.

In spite of all the disturbances Madeleine has found her ideal cottage to be friendly, cosy and warm. Still full of surprises, though. She has twice seen the ghost of a small black dog in the kitchen, once while sitting making a sandwich and another time when she was standing there.

But she maintains that as long as the ghost or ghosts do not get too unruly there is room for them all. Her close friend Jackie is quite used to them, too.

These days, when Jackie arrives at the cottage she goes straight upstairs into her bedroom to say hello to everybody. She doesn't even wait to put her bag down, she goes straight to the room and cheerfully says, 'Hello, hello, I'm here!'

Calling in the Clergy

The Bishop of Shrewsbury arrived in full ceremonial robes accompanied by two priests, one carrying an incense burner. Together they entered the rambling old house at Coton Hill, Shrewsbury.

In the kitchen the table was covered with a white cloth and the three clerics knelt before it in prayer, after which they moved through every room of the house in a ceremony of blessing, the Bishop (the Rt. Rev. William Parker) exhorting everything evil to depart the premises.

The parish priest had called upon the help of the Bishop after spending a night in the haunted house with a worried father and his four children. During four frightening weeks electrical wiring in the house had been ripped out in the middle of the night, wardrobes had been overturned and clothing scattered, a Bible was torn to pieces in a bedroom and there were scores of other unexplained incidents. Most nights the family also saw a dark shape which gave off a smell described as being so repulsive as to be unbelievable.

The constant shocks had proved too much for the wife, who was expecting another child. She had gone away to a maternity hospital. Even the family's Alsatian dog refused to stay in the house at night.

Happily, whatever dark force had held the two hundred-year-old house in its grip was driven away by the

Bishop's ceremony, allowing the family to enjoy their first complete night's rest for a month.

Such calls on the clergy by distressed families are far from rare and the hauntings are not only in old properties. A vicar in Reading, Berkshire, was called to help a family of five in a council house, where a ghost had terrorised them for four months.

The family had only been in the house a week when the wife, Mrs Pat Morley, first saw the hazy figure of a grey-haired old lady in the kitchen. It vanished after a few seconds. Mrs Morley could not believe her eyes, she thought she was 'going bonkers', and she and her husband had a good laugh about it.

But that was only the start, for the apparition returned, and this time more solid. Mrs Morley saw the spectral old lady at least ten more times, as plainly as a living person. Her teenage son also saw the ghost several times. Her husband did not see it but could sense its presence. Once, the living room filled with an overpowering scent of flowers. A few seconds later his wife saw the ghost and told him it was in the room. When it vanished, so did the flowery smell.

One night when Mrs Morley went upstairs as usual to tuck her two young girls into bed she had the severe shock of seeing the old lady's ghost come straight through the wall. That did it. They were all so frightened that for five weeks, before the vicar took a hand, she and her husband and the girls all slept together on mattresses in the living room, while their son slept in another downstairs room with the light on all night.

Neighbours told the harassed family that an elderly woman had died in the house about five years ago. Their description of the woman matched exactly that of the ghost.

The local vicar, the Rev. Arthur Lloyd-Davies, obtained special permission from his bishop to conduct a service of blessing in the house to release its troubled spirit. After the service he visited every room, scattering drops of holy water and saying prayers. It was the first time he had conducted such a ceremony but it seemed to work, as colleagues had told him these services generally did. (Sometimes, incidentally, these services are referred to as services of exorcism, which they are not. A service of blessing aims to give release to an earthbound spirit; to exorcise it would be to consign it to oblivion, which is against Church teaching and practised only in extreme cases.)

The ghost that another vicar was called to deal with was considerably older than the Reading ghost; some one hundred and fifty years old, in fact. This case comes from the 1950s and features a resolute job of rescue by Canon Frank Tucker Harvey, of St Michael's, Ipswich. His notes and those of others give us a detailed account of the affair.

The haunting was at a house near the docks in Ipswich where there lived a merchant seaman, Cecil 'Tug' Wilson, his wife and three young children. It was a sixteenth-century, oak-beamed house that had been the home of generations of seamen, and it seemed that for some reason, the shade of one of the previous tenants resented the Wilson family's intrusion.

The sudden haunting began two weeks before Christmas. The Wilsons' eldest daughter, Penny, aged eight, told her parents that during the night she saw a man 'much taller than Daddy' wearing a white shirt and blue trousers. From her description the ghost had the appearance of a seaman of Nelson's day. The next night and every night afterwards, all night long, there were thumpings and creakings, lights coming on and going off, and weird shadows on the wall. The ghost threw toys, brushes, shoes and a candlestick, and turned out the contents of a drawer. It threw a nailbrush at Mrs Wilson and an antique china boat at her husband as he came downstairs. A cribbage board untouched by anybody came hurtling down the stairs from the attic.

A policeman made several calls at the house but could do little to help the family, now terrified out of their wits by the antagonistic spirit, so they looked to the Church.

Seasonal snow was falling as Canon Tucker Harvey trudged half a mile to the haunted house, where he was greeted by the frightened family and the policeman. The flying cribbage board was still at the foot of the stairs when he arrived. In the ages-old living room he offered up a prayer, in the course of which he prayed 'that God Almighty, who has power over all things, will turn away this evil spirit which is terrifying His children.'

As the Canon returned home through the snow the family decided to sleep together in one room that night. It was just as well they did, for after the cleric's visit the ghost, though subdued, was still active. There were more moving lights and shadows and powder was scattered, pictures were moved, a folded screen was opened out and a child's ball was shifted from one room to another. But at least there was no more hurling of objects, as on other nights. Spiritualists who visited the house said they believed the ghost was that of someone who in life was deprived of family life and was jealous of the Christmas preparations the Wilson family were making.

Undaunted, Canon Tucker Harvey resolved to finish the job. If the souls of his parishioners were disturbed, he said, he felt it was his duty to dispel or quell that disturbance. He thereupon returned to the house, this time donning canonical robes for a full service.

With the family gathered in the gas-lit living room, heads bowed, he offered up this special prayer:

'Almighty and ever loving Father, who knowest every human need, and dost discern the hearts of all men, look in Thy mercy, we pray Thee, on this home and all the members of this family. Drive from amongst them and from this home all signs of spiritual wickedness in dark places.

'Thou hast promised to give Thy beloved peace and so we ask You to grant that as these, Thy children, seek Thy peace, they may have the realisation of Thy loving presence and may know that through their love of Thee all fears and causes of fear will be dispersed. For we know that with Thee all things are possible and that Thou art able to do exceedingly abundantly all that we ask or think. So we pray through Jesus Christ Our Lord.'

The Canon then announced his intention of staying the night. While the family tried to get some rest he kept vigil, spending some time in each of the six rooms of the house, including the attic, fortifying himself with a little whisky and water. To everyone's relief, including his own, he saw and heard nothing and left, satisfied, at 7.30 a.m.

For good measure a seance was held in the house later, after which it was declared free of ghosts. Apart from a final one or two incidents, the Wilsons were able to sleep and enjoy their Christmas and Canon Tucker Harvey to concentrate on his seasonal services at St Michael's.

Two clergymen joined forces to tackle the ghost in a council house in a Suffolk village. A mother of two young daughters, whose husband worked on night shift, was driven to despair when left alone at night to cope with the ghost or poltergeist which haunted the main bedroom. It sent shelves crashing to the floor and clothes floating about the room. The family constantly heard strange noises and were subjected to 'eerie sensations'. The Rev. Ian Davidson, of the village of Great Cornard, called in a colleague from another parish, near Colchester, to help him with a religious service to free the family of the troublesome spirit which forced mother and daughters out of the house to sleep at the home of a married son.

The haunting of an old terraced house in Hull, Yorkshire, in 1969 resulted in a 'task force' of six clergymen being set up to help families in similar distress. The haunting here consisted of frequent appearances of the ghost of a tall, elderly woman wearing a shawl. She was seen many times, just standing there, in the house occupied by demolition worker John Windley, his wife and six children. His wife saw the apparition; so did their thirteen-year-old daughter. So, too, did a friend, who was found rooted to the spot after her experience, hands to her face; her rescuer did not see the ghost but felt its cold, clammy presence while having to pull the friend forcibly from the room. The Windley family, too frightened to sleep upstairs, stayed together in the living room. A psychic the family consulted left the house in some agitation. When the Rev. Thomas Willis, of St Paul's, Hull, took a hand and spent a night in the house he reported experiencing 'a distinctly eerie feeling, a tingling sensation and a chill down the spine'.

The ghost was ultimately identified as being that of a resident of the house half a century ago, who lost her husband soon after marriage and who had died in old age without family; the description of the restless apparition fitted her exactly. She was said to have been a very religious person. After endeavouring to give her soul earthly release, Mr Willis went on to lead his Church 'task force' in dispelling other hauntings.

At this time, two churchmen were called upon to deal with a particularly frightening haunting at a lonely farmhouse in Devon, whose new occupants experienced a mysterious type of paralysis. The malignant, 'intensely evil' spirit manifested itself only days after Mr Tony Cross, his wife, Janet, and their two young children moved into the farmhouse at Huntsham Barton, near Bampton. It struck first at Mr Cross, who was suddenly immobilised for a minute, totally unable to speak or move. He did not tell his wife as he did not at first connect the physical attack with the supernatural, but soon afterwards she underwent the same paralysing experience and they both realised that something very strange was happening.

Mrs Cross then heard footsteps outside her door at night. At first she thought it was her young son, and went back to sleep. Two hours later she awoke to find herself immobilised and unable to speak. Her husband suffered the same paralysing attack. She watched him try to speak to her, but he could do no more than make sounds in the back of his throat. After a few minutes the feeling passed.

The terrified couple, worried about the effect on their children, sought the help of the vicar of Bampton, the Rev. Richard Coath. He investigated the background of the house but could find nothing to suggest that anything unpleasant had ever happened there. Yet although he found the farmhouse to be a 'very cheerful' place, there was a definite feeling of evil there. An authority on the supernatural, the Rev. Sir Patrick Ferguson-Davie, honorary chaplain to the Bishop of Exeter, was now called upon to help. He reported that the unseen force seriously disturbing the family seemed to have the same effect as an electric shock but did not appear to be of the poltergeist variety. He decided that he and the vicar should try to bring an atmosphere of Christianity to the house by means of intensive prayer.

However, on the same evening that Sir Patrick performed a special service at the farmhouse and sprinkled rooms with holy water, Mrs Cross found three photographs lying face down on a bedroom chest of drawers. She knew they could not have fallen because they had been standing at an angle and would have slipped backwards. Following this, the family moved into another part of the house in order to escape the attentions of the 'unhappy spirit' and things were quiet for a time. Then one night, the couple both felt the paralysing sensations again. They contacted Mr Coath, who held communion in the bedroom and lent the couple a crucifix. But the sensations still happened again, the feeling of evil remained in the house and the two churchmen had to redouble their efforts to rid it of its malevolent spirit.

A Staffordshire vicar was called to help combat another spirit that took to physical assault. This was not in a big, old house but in a two-up, two-down cottage. Tough ex-farmer Ivan Woods, who was in his fifties, had lived alone in the cottage at Longnor since his mother died. Three months after her death there the ghost that created pandemonium arrived.

It began one winter's night. Ivan was in bed when he heard a tremendous crash from the other bedroom, which had been used by his mother, followed by a ripping, explosive noise. He went to investigate but everything in the room was normal. However, that was the start of months of unrest for Ivan, who hardly ever got a decent night's sleep, constantly hearing noises 'like someone rolling a giant barrel up and down the stairs', and rumblings in the chimney. He saw calendars and pictures ripped off the wall and chairs moved across the floor on their own. All this was bad enough, but then the spirit became aggressive. Ivan was gripped by powerful unseen hands in the kitchen and one night was pitched bodily out of bed.

Ivan called in his local vicar to stop the ghost driving him from his home and out of his wits. The Rev. E. H. Finnemore held a special service of blessing and prayers, also attending to each room in the little cottage. The haunting began to ease, but once again it took some time to fully subside.

Another haunted cottage, this time near Guildford, Surrey, drew the attentions of a cousin of the Queen, the Rev. Andrew Elphinstone, Rector of Worplesdon. He was called to the farm cottage to deal with a white shrouded figure troubling a young couple with two children. The wife, in her twenties, told how she several times saw the shrouded figure and heard a voice calling her name. A bedroom would feel suddenly cold and there was a curious flickering in the cold grate. Bedclothes were disturbed and she felt her cardigan being tugged.

The white figure was also seen by a number of people as they sat listening to the radio in the cottage. One of them resolved to go to Mr Elphinstone for help. It was the first time the Rector had been involved in anything of the kind, but the family was clearly disturbed and he decided to perform a ceremony of prayer.

The wife believed the ghost to be that of her blind father, who had died three months ago. After the Rector's visit she had a vivid dream in which she felt that her father was trying to reassure her. The family called the Rector in again, and this time his ministration had the desired effect, the disturbances ceasing a day or two later.

Sometimes the work of the clergy has to be directed towards their own house. Such was the case concerning a Worcestershire rectory, where an evil spirit kept the rector awake by howling, screaming, slamming doors and throwing articles about. The Malvern rectory was reputed to have been haunted for centuries. Its ghostly occupant had lately taken to appearing at least once a month and sometimes every night for two or three weeks.

A group of six churchpeople determined to lay the ghost once and for all. Their first investigation of the rectory indicated what they were up against. After they had searched the rectory thoroughly and shut all the windows before keeping vigil, a series of uncanny noises began, a saucepan lid flew up from the kitchen to an upstairs landing and all the metal stair-rods on one flight of stairs shot out.

It was obvious that a united effort would be needed to dispel the haunting. The group of six, consisting of a bishop, an opthalmic surgeon, a Church Army sister and three other women, began a resolute campaign of prayer. They went on to pray for several months. And the power of their prayers won through. The rectory was finally cleared of its disruptive spirit.

That case comes from the 1950s, but little changes in the ghost world, as evidenced by a *Sunday Telegraph* report in 1997. This concerned three Church of England priests who, succeeding each other in a Cambridge vicarage, had been haunted by the ghost of a young woman.

The haunting went on over a period of thirty years. The ghost was first sighted in the 1960s when Canon Bill Loveless moved into St Mark's Vicarage. He heard doors banging inexplicably and the sound of objects being dragged around. Then his wife, Betty, saw the figure of a young girl beside her bed.

After twenty years Canon Loveless was succeeded by Canon Philip Spence, who also soon experienced strange goings-on. He and his wife found the ghost useful in laying out doilies and assisting with dinner placements. The ghost was always doing helpful things in the house, Mrs Spence said, and they did not feel at all frightened.

After the Spences, Canon Christine Farrington arrived at St Mark's in March 1996. No one had said anything to her about the haunting. She said: 'I first came here when the house was empty and was put off because I saw this rather mournful young woman looking out of an upstairs window. I now realise there was no one there. There is no feeling of malevolence, no sense of violence, just of someone being a bit lost.'

The three canons went on local television to discuss their ghostly experiences.

For one man of the cloth, however, a short brush with a rectory ghost proved too much. He reportedly quit the haunted sixteenth-century rectory at Polstead, Suffolk, after spending just five eventful nights there in 1979. The problem created by his abrupt departure was judiciously solved by selling off the big old building to a businessman and installing the next incumbent in a new house built in the village.

The Creep of Camberwell

Two policemen sat on guard in a darkened flat, truncheons and torches ready, listening for the mysterious 'Creep of Camberwell'. At midnight precisely they heard the noises which for a fortnight had scared the occupants – six knocks on the wall followed by heavy footsteps up the stairs. They rushed out and charged, with truncheons held high.

It happened at a house in Camberwell, south London, in the flat of a young mother and her son, aged three. Locked in one of the three rooms of the flat, Mrs Kathleen Crowall sat on a bed while the policemen waited. Downstairs, in another flat, two old ladies were also locked in.

The police vigil began at 10.15 p.m. Acting-Sergeant Leonard Hynds and PC Ronald Bowman went into the sitting room. The whole house, eighty years old and three storeys high, became silent.

This was Sergeant Hynds' report:

'We got tense. At midnight we heard the sounds Mrs Crowall complained about. First there were six knocks on the wall of the room, and while we were investigating we heard a man's footsteps mount the fifteen-odd stairs and stop outside the door. We raised our truncheons, switched on our torches, flung the door open and charged. We expected to find someone creeping about. Instead of that we found nobody, just a silent, deserted staircase.

'Immediately PC Bowman and I searched the house from top to bottom. We went into the attic, unlocked the old ladies' flat and questioned them, and went downstairs into an unoccupied, furnished flat. We found nothing to account for the noises. It was baffling.'

Mrs Crowall refused to stay in the house any longer and was taken by the officers to a London County Council home for the night. With her went her little son, Bernard, the child who started the mystery. Mrs Crowall said in her statement to the police: 'A fortnight ago he woke up screaming in the night, saying that he had seen a light and the figure of a man standing in the bedroom. I believe it must be something to do with the ghost of an old man who died in the flat before I moved in.'

The next night, as mother and child stayed away, four policemen kept watch on the house in deserted, rainy Sultan Street, while inside, an intrepid reporter from the *Daily Mail* lay in wait for the sinister 'Creep of Camberwell'. And it happened again, at 11.37 p.m.

'Above the noise of the wind there came suddenly six knocks, heavy and echoing in the old house. Then followed sounds of footsteps walking quickly but softly across the attic floor above me. They stopped, to be followed by a scraping noise, suggesting that the attic trap door above the kitchen was being raised. Then all was silent again. Cautiously I flashed a torch round the toy-strewn room. Then I opened the door to the kitchen. It was deserted. The attic door remained firmly closed. The bedroom was empty and silent.'

Immediately the sounds were heard the watching policemen entered the house. By flashlight they searched the staircase, kitchen, cubicles and sitting room. They found nothing.

Police continued to keep a watchful eye on the house pestered by the 'Creep' until the haunting finally subsided, to remain on police books as one of those peculiar unexplained mysteries, as did another bizarre haunting which happened around the same time in the 1950s, also in south London. This was at a council-requisitioned house in west Norwood where, one night, no fewer than nine policemen lay in wait, ready to pounce on the faceless phantom that was terrorising a family.

This haunting had actually had its beginnings four years earlier. Six months after moving into the house in Langmead Street, the Greenfield family began to hear mysterious tappings in the empty loft. Birds or mice were suspected, though nothing was found. Gradually the noises grew louder, until they sounded like coal being broken and furniture dragged. But there was neither coal nor furniture in the loft.

Then came the night when the ghost manifested itself. Cecil Greenfield, one of the family's two grown-up sons, was asleep in his first-floor bedroom when he was suddenly awakened by odd sounds of movement outside the bedroom door. On going out on to the landing to investigate he was appalled to see rounding a bend in the stairs a tall, grey-white, faceless shape, its arms folded across its breast. It slowly advanced upwards towards him and he was conscious of an icy coldness creeping nearer. As the shape passed over a loose board there was a creak as would have been made by a solid person. It was almost within touching distance when Cecil finally found his voice and shouted out. Instantly the shape vanished, his parents rushing out to find him white and shaken.

The phantom's second appearance came soon afterwards. The Greenfields' other son, Dennis, and his wife, arriving home late after an evening out, opened the front door and were petrified to see the same six-foot tall, grey-white, faceless figure standing in the narrow hall, this time with its arms hung at its sides. They ran in panic to a neighbour's house, and when they all rushed back together the spectre had vanished.

When the phantom appeared a third time, this time to the Greenfields' teenage daughter, in the afternoon, in desperation the family called the police.

Officers maintained vigils under the direction of Inspector Sidney Candler, culminating in the peak night when nine of them lay in wait. On hearing raps and thumps coming from the loft, several policemen squeezed through the trap door, the only means of entry and exit, but found nothing and no one. Meanwhile, elsewhere in the six-roomed house an eiderdown was moved from a bed and a picture crashed from a wall, the cord unbroken and the nail firmly in place. Inspector Candler, a sceptic when the police operation commenced, was speedily convinced that something strange was happening, something his officers were powerless to deal with.

Once, after the police had left, teacups in the kitchen were unaccountably moved, a spoon in a sugar basin in a closed cupboard was heard rattling, a large photograph fell from its frame, leaving the glass front and cardboard backing undisturbed, and a shopping basket was flung from the unoccupied living room.

One afternoon, returning home from shopping to an empty house, Mrs Greenfield found a married daughter and a newspaperman awaiting her on the doorstep. They told of hearing heavy thumps from inside. When they entered, furniture had been moved about and a hanging mirror turned to the wall.

On entering his young sister's bedroom while she was out, Dennis Greenfield was alarmed to see her mattress lifting and curling up as if moved by invisible hands. He tried to push it down but could make no impression on it. Then an invisible something seized him from behind, tearing his shirt.

The initials 'A.T.' were found written in the attic dust, mysterious kiss marks were found on the glass of a wardrobe, and a crucifix on a dressing table was turned upside down. Brilliant luminous flashes were seen in the living room by all members of the family.

Afraid to go upstairs after dark the family moved beds

to a ground-floor room, but did not sleep. When the police vigils proved useless the distressed family sought shelter at night with friends, but the next unfortunate turn of events saw crowds gathered outside the house each evening and into the small hours, gazing up at the windows or knocking at the door with requests to be allowed to look over the haunted rooms. Police had to restrain some sightseers from forcing their way into the house. However, after weeks of uproar the west Norwood phantom finally ceased its activities, to remain as yet another unsolved mystery on police files. The haunted Greenfield family eventually moved out and, as in so many cases, the new tenants were never troubled.

It was 1.30 a.m. on an October night in 1960 when a frightened family of six surged into Walworth police station in London to tell the duty officer that they had fled their council flat because it was haunted by evil spirits. Mr Harold Titus, his wife Agnes and their four children under fifteen had dashed out of their ground-floor flat in Peckham, leaving the lights on and all their possessions inside. It was duly noted that 'the whole family was shaking with terror and the oldest boy (aged fourteen) was nearly hysterical'.

The police tried to calm the family, sending a constable round to the flat to investigate. He reported that the lights were still on and all was quiet. The family, however, refused to return to their haunted home and went to stay the night with friends.

The Tituses, who had only been in the flat for three months, complained about spirits in their living room, kitchenette, bathroom and three bedrooms. The frightening incidents included weird knockings on the wall at midnight, a heavy mirror leaping off the wall and crashing to the floor, a smashed clock and a shattered electric lamp, the glass from its bulb showering over the oldest boy's bed with the lamp's plastic shade ripped to shreds. Things had reached a climax that night when the parents woke up to hear the boy screaming. There was a terrible banging and thumping, then their daughter, aged ten, woke up screaming too, and the noise of banging and crashing seemed to be all round them. Even after they had got the boy up in his wrecked bedroom, where the bedclothes were scattered about and the whole room in disorder, he seemed to be in a trance and holding his head. The father decided that was it, they had to get out. They stopped only to put coats on over their nightclothes, after which he bundled them into the car and drove to the nearest police station.

The father returned to the police the day after their night flight to ask if the law could arrange for a priest to get rid of the spirits. The police thought such a task was hardly their province, but they could look at the facts, and what emerged was that the father had recently become interested in spiritualism and had attended seances. Moreover, only a few days ago he and two friends had held a seance in the flat.

The right solution seemed clear, and it was taken. The family sought the help of a local medium who, with an assistant, moved from room to room with the flat in darkness apart from a blue light, trying to make contact with the ghost that had been aroused. It was believed to be that of a man who was murdered in one of the houses which stood on the site before the Blitz. The medium was able to extract a promise from the spirit that it would give no further trouble, and the family returned to their flat in peace, the father vowing he had finished dabbling in spiritualism for good.

Unfortunately, many cases on police books are not easily tidied up. The case of 'Tottenham Fred' is one such. In the late 1960s two policemen from Tottenham police station in London were highly sceptical when called to a council flat in the area to investigate a report of a ghost. But their attitude soon changed when they heard for themselves strange rappings on the wall and tappings on the floor, and they could not believe their eyes when part of a bedroom wall bulged out at least six inches and no one was on the other side of it.

A third policeman also heard the strange noises. Sergeant Bernard Taffs reported: 'There was a thumping on the walls and all the windows were rattling. I do not believe in ghosts but I just cannot explain this.' Nor could anyone else.

'Fred' – the name given to the spirit by the police – had moved in with Stanley Woodbridge, his wife and four children, a week earlier. Since then the family had had sleepless nights as he/it moved from room to room of the flat, banging furiously on walls and floorboards. Already, besides the police officers, more than twenty other people had heard Fred in action, including one man who promptly fainted.

When the police confessed themselves baffled, council officials investigated the flat. They, too, were mystified. There then began a steady stream of experts from the council who carefully examined the entire structure of the building and its surroundings, but they found nothing wrong with it; no one could come up with a rational explanation for the disturbances. One theory, that an underground river flowed below the house and was causing the building to move, was quickly disproved.

And that was only the start. Fred carried on his activities for several months. Besides the bangings and rappings, the ghost's antics included light bulbs being taken out of their sockets, a heavy bookcase shifted, and books, shoes and clothes being mysteriously thrown about. The constant banging made a hole in the wall of a teenage son's bedroom, and once, the lad was in bed when it was suddenly moved violently across the room. As his father testified, 'The tricks Fred gets up to are fantastic. We've even whistled a tune and had him tap-dancing on the linoleum. I used to get angry with him and call him names,

but that only made him worse. Now I try to humour him.'
It got so bad that his wife, nervous and strained through
lack of sleep, had to go and stay with a married daughter
for a time. The family concluded that Fred was harmless
but he was a thorough nuisance, and their only recourse
was to ask the council to rehouse them. Neighbours said
there had been a number of deaths in the flat before the
Woodbridges moved in, but noisy Fred was never
identified.

Police were called to the rescue of two terror-stricken girls
in their flat in London's Kensington Church Street. The
sisters from South Africa had never given a thought to
ghosts, but all that changed one summer's night in 1970.
   The trouble started at three o'clock in the morning,
when the heavy couch one of the girls was sleeping on
suddenly swung across the room with great violence. Then
vases shot across the room and smashed against the wall.
Ashtrays and cushions were sent floating through the air.
   As usual, police looked for possible physical causes for
the upset, but there were none. A fingerprint expert could
find no prints on objects which the girls had seen hurled
across the room. Finally, the landlady called in a medium.
She found that the place was haunted by a child who had
died in tragic circumstances. The trouble, she said, was all
due to a pop art painting which one of the girls had just
bought; it had thoroughly upset the ghost child.
   The sisters were not disposed to argue. They burned
the painting and quit the flat for another half a mile away.

The sounds of a baby crying in an empty room ... footsteps
on the stairs ... peculiar smells wafting through the house
... more strange noises ... and then the startling
appearance of the ghost of a white-bearded, pipe-smoking
sea captain, accompanied by the strong smell of his tobacco
... it all finally proved too much for a young husband, his
wife and her mother at the mother's house in Isleworth,

Middlesex. They called the police who, finding the family 'in a state of great distress', went inch by inch over walls and through cupboards in the ten-roomed house and also pulled up floorboards, but found nothing to account for the noises and smells. It was a cold January night, but Mrs Barbara Basted locked up her haunted house and she, her daughter and son-in-law left to spend the night trying to get some sleep in a railway station waiting room.

Mrs Basted told the police that her daughter and her husband had laughed at first when she told them about the ghostly noises she had heard so often, but now they were convinced. Her daughter refused to go back to the house and, the mother said, the three of them were getting out once and for all.

What must be the most curious ghostly case on Cambridgeshire police records occurred at Chatteris in the winter of 1968. Mr Fred Brown, a young agricultural worker, moved into a terraced house with his wife and two sons at the end of December. He passed it off as a joke when, within weeks, his sons, aged five and four, complained that the neighbours in the house next door 'looked like monsters' when they spotted them through the back bedroom window. But he changed his mind when he heard the odd sound of a man and woman talking. Then he saw a woman with a child through a window and one night heard a voice crooning softly and a baby crying. He called the police. The house next door was full of ghosts, he told them. There were tappings on the wall, shadows in the windows and strange noises in the night. None of his family would sleep unless the lights were left on.

The police investigated – only to find that the haunted house was quite empty and had been unoccupied for a whole year. It was recorded: 'We investigated Mr Brown's complaint but could find nothing officially wrong'.

The frightened family were left with finding another house, and the sooner the better.

Ghosts All His Life

Charles Crundwell has seen ghosts all his life. He was nineteen years old when he saw his first one. It was the image of a youth of about his own age, in a white laboratory coat and holding two phials, one in each hand, and smiling.

Charles thought he was going mad. He went straight to his doctor, who told him: 'No, you are not going mad. It is simply that you are psychic.'

Since that time Charles has seen ghosts by the hundred. Not that he has ever fancied himself as a ghost-hunter or an investigator of the paranormal. He does not go seeking ghosts; they come to him. And the disconcerting thing is that he never knows who they are; they're always complete strangers to him.

Charles explains: 'They are not white and ghostly when I see them. They are not transparent. They all appear to me as normal people of flesh and blood, with one difference. Each one I see looks like a subject in one of those old-fashioned sepia-coloured photographs, bathed in an aura of glowing, golden brown. I have seen so many people that way, but they are never people I know. If they were, I could perhaps explain that it was my subconscious wish that they should appear. Sometimes they are Chinese or coloured people. Always the features are animated, and the image lasts about half a minute to a minute.'

Two things must be said right away about Charles Crundwell. One, experts of the most responsible psychic research bodies have investigated his claims and are convinced of his integrity. And two, he has by no means waited around to see his multitude of ghosts, having led a hard and busy life in the theatre. He was, in fact, an adagio dancer.

Charles danced with his lovely wife, Grace. They were known as Carl and Colette. Sometimes they would have six girls working with them, when they would be billed as Carl and Colette and the Debonaires. It was a strenuous life touring the country in the 1930s; a matinée and two evening performances, three shows a day. Sometimes, in addition to their act, they would also look after the company's wardrobe, some three hundred costumes. They would pack up the wardrobe on the Saturday night, ready for the train call next day, everyone meeting at the station ready to depart for the next town on the tour. Not much time to spend thinking about ghosts, but they appeared to him just the same. Once, staying with friends in south London, he asked them: 'Who is that young lad who keeps running in and out?' It was a boy of eight or nine with distinctive brown eyes, large and lustrous. 'Are *you* at it now?' said his friends. They confessed that other visitors had also seen the boy, although they themselves could not.

Charles began to experiment with an Ouija board in the hope that he might develop his psychic powers, but several things happened that made him abandon the idea. On one occasion the table round which they were sitting, and on which the Ouija board rested, rose up and pinned his wife into the fireplace. Fortunately there was no fire on at the time. At another sitting they were trying to get the answers to questions when the glass spelt out 'You should know better than that', whipped up and smashed itself against the wall. After that he gave up.

'The trouble with the Ouija board,' he told me, 'was that I could make it say anything I wanted it to say.

However, I did think there was some outside influence at work at times and one I did not understand. So I left it alone.'

Besides the constant sighting of ghosts there were other curious incidents. The Crundwells had a close friend who sat in at rehearsals and would also be in the audience at their shows, but one day he had to go up country. That night Charles remarked to his wife that it would be strange without their friend in the audience, but during the performance he sensed the friend standing on the stage watching him. Surprise confirmation of this came when the pianist said to Crundwell afterwards: 'Did you see anything tonight? I sensed a man on the stage with you.' The pianist was the well-known George Shearing, the blind performer.

Charles's wife did not see the ghosts, although she could sense things at times. However, their theatrical career demanded undivided attention, especially when working with snakes. Charles and Grace occasionally appeared with pythons wrapped around their necks. The snakes were heavy but warm and dry; Grace loved them and enjoyed appearing with them, but Charles was terrified. Their owner would keep an eye on the snakes from the rear, whispering to them to keep still and checking that they were not tiring after the long day's shows; he could see from the way their jaws were moving if they were threatening to bite – and pythons have rows and rows of very sharp teeth.

Charles and Grace Crundwell gave up their theatrical career shortly after the Second World War. In 1953, in his early forties, Charles took the tenancy of a pub in the village of Icklesham, Sussex. And, as might be expected, he soon discovered that the old place had a resident ghost.

The Queen's Head was then just an old beer house, not much changed from when it was built in 1763, when George III was on the throne. It was in very poor condition and the Crundwells found the prospect of restoring it so daunting that after only a month they considered pulling out. But they didn't, they stayed. With a lot of hard work they transformed it from a rundown old beer house into a complete pub, a decent place with a lovely atmosphere. Charles eventually bought it from the brewery and it remained their home and business for twenty-five years.

And George's. He was the ghost, and he made his presence felt shortly after the Crundwells moved in.

In an upstairs room where Charles kept the spirits – the liquor kind – he was several times possessed of a weird feeling that he could not leave the room. He would enter it, do his work, then find it almost impossible to walk out. At length he used to say to the unseen force apparently demanding his attention: 'Leave me alone, I've got to get on with it!' and he would force himself out of the room.

He did not want to involve himself with the ghostly inhabitant, but it persisted. There was a little brass knocker on one of the bedroom doors and this began to rattle and bang in the middle of the night. People staying with them heard it too, telling Charles: 'Somebody was playing japes last night, because the knocker kept knocking.'

Then the ghost manifested itself. Charles had been at the pub about six months when he first saw old George sitting there, dressed in an old countryman's smock. After that the ghost appeared at intervals, and not only to Charles.

There was the day a woman friend of theirs came in and told them: 'There's a man in the bar waiting to be served.' When Charles went to investigate there was nobody there. She had seen old George. So, in the course of time, did several other people. Charles himself saw the old man at intervals, and when he did not see him he was nevertheless aware of him many, many times. Grace also sensed George moving about, though she never saw him. George's favourite haunt was the bar room, where he would sit in a high-backed Windsor chair; wherever the chair was moved to he would find it and he would be seen sitting there looking into the fire.

George got his name after inquiries established his probable identity. He was thought to be a former landlord of the Queen's Head, a farm worker who had the old beer house from about 1870 till dying there in 1890. His name was George Gutsell, and he was given a great send-off by relatives and customers. They hoisted his coffin up on to the bar counter and drank to his health in the hereafter.

George the ghost brought many a visitor to the Queen's Head. They included psychic investigators, the plain curious, and even a student writing a thesis; plus, of course, the inevitable film people. There was a Dutch film, and a BBC film, which mostly had to make do with showing things like a cat stalking in menacing fashion across the bar floor. George, like many other ghosts, had no time for film producers.

The Crundwells sold the Queen's Head in 1977, retiring to a cottage barely a stone's throw away.

George the ghost had his sceptics, of course, and on occasion answered them smartly. Once, the man who subsequently took over the pub, when told of the ghost, said: 'Oh, I don't believe all of this!' – at which one of a set of heavy little glasses that had belonged to Grace's mother leapt off a shelf and smashed to pieces on the beer pump four feet away. Then, among other things, there was the beer bottle incident. The Crundwells were back at the pub as customers, having a drink, when an acquaintance loudly voiced his disbelief of George. The beer bottle promptly leapt eight feet and slid right down the bar.

Although the interior of the Queen's Head has altered considerably since the Crundwells left, I am told George still occasionally makes his presence felt. Charles Crundwell, now in his eighties, crisp and bright-eyed in retirement, lives with other ghosts; still always strangers, never anyone he knows or knew. He explains quite simply: 'I don't call them ghosts, they are spirits, and I see them all the time. Some people go to bed and read a book. I hop into bed and see spirits, sometimes six at a time.'

The morning I spoke to Charles he had seen five ghosts at once the night before. One, he told me, was a woman with gorgeous eyelashes who smiled at him, then disappeared. And, as with them all, and somewhat to his regret, he had not the faintest idea who she was.

Terror on Holiday

Alice, a young north London housewife, was looking forward to enjoying a very first family holiday with her husband and four young children. This was in the 1950s, when most people still went off to the English seaside; but the question was, just where to take the four little ones? One day, with her husband's holiday date fast approaching, the answer came to Alice's front door.

'I happened to be talking to my laundryman and he told me that he could give me the name of a woman who owned a house at Jaywick Sands, in Essex. She was the daughter of the lady who formerly owned the house and she lived at Cricklewood, not far away, so I phoned her up and went to see her. From what she told me, the house seemed fine for our purposes, so I booked a two weeks' holiday there in August. As it was coming up close to the time we would be going away and we had never been away before – it really was something special – I paid her for the whole holiday there and then.

'The following week when the laundryman came he asked if I had been to see the woman and I told him yes, I had booked up with her. He then proceeded to tell me how he and his wife always went to Jaywick on holiday and they had known the little old lady who used to own the house, which was set back from the sea front. He said the old lady always dressed in black and you could never miss her, she was a familiar sight sitting on the wall at the front. She used to vow that she would never leave Jaywick because she always felt so safe there, and although it was flat, if ever there were any floods she was confident the waters would never reach her home.

'But they did, the laundryman told me, unfortunately, during the great flood of 1952, as the water started to get closer and closer to her house and she had frantically tried to escape by climbing up a stepladder in the kitchen into the loft, but fell in the attempt and died.

'Well, I can't tell you how I felt when he told me the old lady had died in the house. I was devastated. The floods had only happened two years ago and knowing that I would have to be working in the kitchen where the old lady so recently met her tragic end worried me sick. I was not used to death. I had never recovered from the shock of my grandfather's death when I was a little girl. I had never been that close to where someone had died tragically. I had never even been to a funeral.

'I felt very uneasy about it but I didn't dare tell my husband after having paid out all that money for the holiday and I couldn't disappoint the children, who had never been on holiday before. So, worried as I was, I did not say anything about it to anybody.

'We finally went off to Jaywick; my husband and I, our four children, the oldest just seven years old, and my young sister. When we got there the house seemed nice enough, clean and comfortable, although I was still uneasy about it, a feeling which was not helped by the behaviour of Jimmy, aged three and a half, when I was putting him to bed that first night. Jimmy was very fond of his toy cowboy guns in their holsters and wore them a lot. As I was getting him ready for bed he didn't want to take his guns off. I said, "You've got to take them off, you can't go to bed with them. What do you want to take them to bed with you for anyway?"

"Well," he said, "I want to shoot the ghosts if they come."

'It was such a strange thing for him to say. I told him not to be silly, there were no such things as ghosts, but I did allow him to tuck one of the guns under his pillow.

'The next morning at breakfast, Jimmy gave me the shock of my life when he suddenly said, "Mummy, I saw your grandmother last night."

'My heart skipped a beat but I tried to keep calm. "What do you mean?" I said.

'"Well," he said, "she was a little old lady dressed in black."

'I nearly died as he said it, for it was the exact description the laundryman had given me of the old lady and there was no way any of the children could have known this. I tried to pass it off although it really shook me, and my fears were not helped by what my husband said the next day. The house had an outside toilet reached down a small alleyway lying between the side of the house and the church or chapel which stood next door. My husband said it gave him the creeps going down this alleyway at night; his hair actually stood on end. This happened every time he visited the toilet after dark, even though there was some light outside.

'After all this I was terribly nervous and edgy, which made me constantly bad-tempered. My husband could not understand what was wrong with me. I kept telling him I wanted to go home. On the ninth day he got really angry and said, "Why are you acting like this? You wanted to come away, but now you want to go home. Why are you acting so funny? What's the matter with you?" I then told him what the laundryman had said to me about the old lady dying in the kitchen and how his description of her tied up exactly with what young Jimmy had seen.

'I did not have to start packing; my husband went into the bedroom and started it for me. We left for home the next day. Our holiday still had four days to run, but we neither of us worried about that.'

A Ghost at the Bank

One of the fascinations of the real ghost world, as opposed to the fictional one, is the way ghosts can turn up in the most unlikely places. Anywhere and everywhere, in fact. Here are some examples.

Every schoolboy knows of the fate of Admiral John Byng, a predecessor of Captain Bligh. His failure to relieve Minorca from siege by the French resulted in court martial and execution. That was in 1757. Did the luckless Admiral return more than two hundred years later, in 1993?

It was thought that a ghost seen at the Royal Naval College, Greenwich, in the house of Admiral Sir Michael Layard, Second Sea Lord, could well be that of Byng. The ghost, dressed in a black and gold uniform, was reported to have been spotted on the grand central staircase of the Admiral President's House, and to have given Admiral Layard and his wife some restless nights. The family's springer spaniel was seen to drop his ball in alarm for no apparent reason. A woman steward carrying a tray looked up the grand staircase to see a man dressed in black, 'with gold on his shoulders'.

Byng, who was in his early fifties, commanded a British fleet sent to the Mediterranean to relieve the island of Minorca, but after an inconclusive engagement with the French, withdrew to Gibraltar. Minorca fell, Byng was arrested at Spithead and held at Greenwich. A court martial found him guilty of negligence and he was executed by firing squad.

Some historians say the unfortunate Admiral would be perfectly justified in haunting Greenwich as they firmly believe the court-martial verdict was a farce.

Banks are not normally the sort of places one associates with ghosts, unless haunted by one's overdraft, but strange things do occur in those austerely practical buildings. Even the Bank of England is said to be haunted by the lingering spirit of an old cashier.

The ghost that appeared at Coutts Bank in the Strand, London – the Queen's bank – was somewhat different. Four members of staff were reported early in 1993 to have had separate encounters with a ghostly figure who left them with an icy chill. Three telephonists saw the wraith wandering about, a mournful figure in doublet and hose. The bank finally called in a psychic investigator, Mr Eddie Burks.

He identified the restless Elizabethan phantom roaming the building as Thomas Howard, Fourth Duke of Norfolk, who was executed for treason in 1572. Howard was a favourite of Elizabeth I, but fell disastrously out of favour when accused of planning to marry Mary Queen of Scots and instal her as Queen. He was only thirty-six when sent to the scaffold. It was a trumped-up charge, the ghostly Duke avowed to the investigator; he had since spent four centuries lamenting the loss of his head and intimated to Mr Burks that he could not obtain release from this world until he had told his story.

The Howards, although a family of some substance and power, were a particularly unfortunate lot, never far from imprisonment or execution (Catherine Howard, Henry VIII's fifth wife, who also lost her head, was one; her ghost haunts Hampton Court Palace, where Henry had her locked up before being taken to the block).

However, for ghostly Thomas Howard his identification brought about a most unusual sequel. Lady Mary Mumford, a family member, was moved to assemble her relations at a Roman Catholic church not far from the bank to pray for the repose of Thomas's soul. So, on a November day in 1993, exactly four hundred and twenty-one years after his execution, a special service was held at Corpus Christi in Maiden Lane, off the Strand; it was an official Howard family thanksgiving for the lives of Thomas and his father, Henry Howard, the poet Earl of Surrey, who also suffered execution. The service included three hymns, a reading and prayers for the dead, after which Mr Burks ascended the sanctuary to describe his encounter with the ghostly Duke who, he said, had thanked him for lifting his burden and disappeared, basked in white radiated heat.

Thomas has troubled the bank no more.

The star of a Gloucestershire pantomime in 1994, backstage, that is, was the ghost of a moody stage manager. Rehearsals for *Snow White and the Seven Dwarfs* at the Phoenix Community Centre, Cirencester, took an alarming turn when a wardrobe mistress found costumes floating around a changing room.

Old hands recalled similar peculiar things happening in the 1970s after the stage manager, Charlie Robinson, dropped dead in the car park. Objects shifted mysteriously, breezes whistled across stage and rooms turned chilly. Now, it seemed, a repeat performance was under way. A flying pole just missed the current stage manager, dogs refused to enter the premises, and a padlock was seen spinning. A photographer was taking a picture of a photo of the late Mr Robinson when books flew out of a bookcase.

Another former stage manager, Ralph Lovell, said Robinson had been a devoted man who loved making scenery. He ruled the roost and had firm views. Somebody must be doing something he didn't like.

Lovell's wife, apparently, had her own brush with Robinson. She once looked over some portraits he had painted. When she remarked that she could have done better herself, an invisible hand gave her a clip round the ear.

A ghost at an auction sale? True enough. Sotheby's have on record a sale at a West Country manor where the peevish spirit of the late owner made such a nuisance of himself, being responsible for numerous alarming noises on the opening day of the sale and a fair bit of unexplained shifting around of the furniture, that it was necessary to seek the help of a local clergyman in protecting the premises, or at any rate in appeasing the ghost, to ensure the auction was a success and that none of the bidders took fright.

Walking the galleries and corridors of the Royal Albert Hall, London, in its quiet periods, as I have done, it is easy to envisage that wonderfully atmospheric Victorian building being an ideal haven for ghosts of yesteryear. That is pure imagination. But the fact is that the hall does appear to have had some resident ghosts for years.

This came to light when work was due to begin on installing new offices there in 1996. Spectral apparitions, weird noises and sudden chills were said to have plagued its corridors for some sixty years. The hall's director of building development said that since the first sighting in the 1930s, workmen and staff in the building during the night had on a number of occasions complained of a 'feeling of unease' and strange noises or a sudden drop in temperature. On nearly every occasion the hall was undergoing some kind of building or repair work. If there were ghostly activities they seemed likely to occur again when night workers started putting in the new offices, so the management decided to call in an investigator of the paranormal.

The last recorded ghostly sighting had been in 1989, in a carpeted basement area beneath the north side of the hall, when a night manager came upon two young women dressed in Victorian clothes. He stated: 'I heard giggling and female talk so I went into the corridor, where I saw the back view of these two women heading towards the kitchen. I went up to them and said, "Excuse me, but you can't go in there, it's out of bounds." They just faded into the blackness.'

The area around the hall's organ is also believed to be haunted by a stooped old man wearing a skull cap who berates workmen whenever work is done on the instrument. This apparition is thought to be that of Henry Willis, the organ's designer and the father of British organ building.

So far as we know, the Albert Hall's ghosts remain comfortably in residence, for it appears little or nothing was found by the investigator and attendant newspapermen, plus of course the inevitable television cameras, which are practically guaranteed to scare away any ghost.

A young American girl student who visited the Tower of London on a December day in 1994 had a big surprise when her holiday snaps were developed back home in Redlands, California. A snap she had taken of Traitors' Gate showed a ghostly glowing hand in the foreground, belonging to someone dressed in a sixteenth-century tunic.

The holiday film had been developed at a local shop and there was no mistaking the spectral arm thrusting in from the right foreground, its hand resting on the wire fence fronting Traitors' Gate. Shannon John had taken the snap with an ordinary camera and had not used a flash. The family had the negative rigorously checked: Kodak confirmed that the image had been taken at the time of the exposure, while an enlargement confirmed the strange quality of the glowing arm.

Miss John recalled that she and a friend were the only

two people in the area at the time she took the snap. There had been something a bit strange, a bit eerie, about the place and now it seemed obvious why. She remembered that it had been quite a warm day, but when she took the picture it suddenly went really cold.

The ghostly photograph was sent to the Tower of London, where, after careful examination, it remained a mystery; yet another to add to the long, long list of mysterious things which have happened within those historic walls.

The case of the haunted ballroom comes from Bishop's Stortford, in Hertfordshire. The manager there, Bill Higley, was convinced that an unseen dancer or dancers took the floor after everyone had gone home. His guard dog, Bosun, also sensed the ghostly activity when they were patrolling at night, sometimes showing quite plainly that he had spotted the intruders. Halfway across the dance floor he would freeze and stand growling with his hair standing on end. There were other incidents, like the night the manager saw the ballroom lights switch themselves on and off. Then he heard a noise from the kitchen, like someone having a wash. When he investigated, the tap had been turned on but there was no one there. The ballroom building dated back to the early eighteenth century and there had been talk in the past about ghosts, but who these latest spectral visitors were remained a mystery.

Not so in the case of a haunted discotheque, for at least the ghost there showed itself. Events happened shortly after the disco was opened below the Vestry pub in Sunderland, a building which dated from Victorian times and had been a men-only venue for the town's top businessmen. After customers had left the disco the ghost of an elderly bearded man in Edwardian clothes was seen to shuffle silently along the bar and vanish through a wall. Four members of staff saw him on different occasions. The first witnesses were the manager and a barman. The manager was standing with his back to the bar when the barman, who was facing him, turned as white as death. The manager turned round in time to see the ghost with a King Edward VII beard vanish through the wall. He was still sceptical until he was alone early one morning and saw the same figure pass along the whole length of the bar and disappear through the wall. Another member of staff was down in the disco with one of the guard dogs when it suddenly howled with fear and the hair rose on its back. There was an eerie sensation and as he and the dog turned for the stairs he caught a glimpse of the bearded ghost. After this neither of the two guard dogs would go near the cellar while the outbreak lasted.

Supermarkets hardly seem to be suitable haunting places for ghosts, but such hauntings do occur, and one at an Asda store in Widnes, Cheshire, in 1994 produced a likely explanation, though not before it had given night staff the jitters.

Such puzzlements as packets of cigarettes mysteriously switching themslves around were one thing, but quite another was the sudden unnatural chattering among a display of teddy bears which only talked when their paws were pressed. The culprit proved to be a grey-cloaked ghost woman who prowled the aisles late at night, often humming as she went. Staff nicknamed her the Singing Lady. Frightened shelf-stackers asked to be allowed to work in pairs.

Customer services manager Ann Taylor was reportedly so scared on seeing the ghost that she transferred to another branch. On coming down from the office one night she saw a shadow passing through the door. She looked again and saw the ghost's head covered by a grey hood.

The cause of the haunting came to light. The

supermarket had been built on the site of a drainage pit where a woman drowned at the turn of the century. Staff were convinced she had come back; the personnel manager said they had all felt her presence. A chilly episode while it lasted.

As varied as the ghosts themselves are the ways in which we get to learn of them.

Friends of ours and their small daughter went to stay at a country hotel in Alfriston, Sussex, for a long weekend. They were the only guests. Young Nona, aged five, got up to go to the toilet first thing in the morning but stopped on seeing a young woman in a long blue dress and white apron go in there first. She ran back to her parents and said she needed to go to the loo, but a lady had gone in before her. Her parents were puzzled, having been told they were the only guests, but asked the little girl to wait a few minutes and then see if the toilet was unoccupied, and this she did.

At breakfast, Nona's parents casually asked the owners about the other guests, only to be told again that they were the only people staying there. But, they said, what about the woman their daughter had seen? and they described her. Oh, they were told, the young woman in the blue dress and apron was in fact a maidservant who was murdered in the eighteenth century and her body put in a settle in the hall. From time to time she got up and walked!

Another friend of ours was driving up from the Sussex coast to north Kent when, just outside the village of Rolvenden, she came upon a young man thumbing a lift.

'I stopped and he said "Canterbury?" I said "Yes, perhaps you can show me the way." He said yes, he had to meet someone at Sturry railway station so he could show me how to get there, and a good job he did, because it was such a convoluted route. He said he was at Canterbury University and was going back early because of some trouble at home. He was then quiet for a time and looked me over before deciding he could tell me more. He said his father was a doctor and had retired early because of ill-health. He bought a cottage locally that had been two cottages but had been knocked into one. Very soon they had found the place to be haunted. His mother had seen this strange woman standing outside the kitchen window when she was peeling potatoes and generally getting the dinner ready. The ghost woman then appeared in his sister's bedroom – every time his sister woke up she was standing there. It was too much for his sister, who left to stay with an aunt in Margate. Then the ghost got on his mother's nerves so much that she, too, had to leave the cottage and was now living with a friend until his father had got rid of it. It was not that the ghost was evil or harming them, he explained, it was just that they were all so scared. Every time he himself walked down to the kitchen and sat at the wooden table, there was the ghost over his back, he could see its reflection. He, too, couldn't stand it any more and that was why he was going back early.

'I can still see that young man's troubled face as I dropped him off at Sturry, and I have often wondered what the poor father had to do to get his frightened family back together again.'

'Old Bob' was a good-looking man, a reliable man, a chapel-going man; he used to play the organ in a little chapel on Sunday. My stonemason friend Jim McGuigan had a lot of respect for old Bob – except when it came to his tale of a ghost, which Jim found hard to swallow. This was in the village of Brightling, Sussex, and if the tale had concerned a ghostly Mad Jack Fuller, the eccentric squire who built follies in the countryside round about, it might have been acceptable. Everyone knew about Mad Jack, supposedly buried in his pyramid-shaped tomb in the churchyard, sitting in a chair with a pint in his hand and broken glass strewn all around to prevent the devil getting to him. But it was not that at all, as Jim McGuigan recalls.

'Old Bob told me about a different kind of ghost, that of a little old Victorian lady who made a walk after sundown. He had seen her, he said, and so had others. She came through the main gate of the parish church, walked down the road for about a hundred yards, maybe a little more, then turned into another gate and vanished. He was very serious about this but I'm afraid I couldn't help laughing. "All right then," he said, "you be here tonight at half past nine, quarter to ten, and we'll have a little walk."

'I turned up on time just to humour him, but then it happened. Out of the main gate came the figure of a little old lady in bonnet, cape and big old skirt and started off down the road. Bob and I were walking side by side and as I looked across she was more or less in line with us. I was shocked and tried to point or something but Bob just said quietly "I know, lad, I know ..." We walked all the way down until we came to a gate, an ordinary wooden gate. She just went through it and that was the last we saw of her.

'I was left in a bit of a state. I drove off in my van and for a good two miles or more I felt a presence in the back, enough to raise the hairs on the back of my neck and make me swear to myself that I would never go back there again. And I never have.'

That incident was in 1980. We now move on to a summer's day in 1995 and a friend walking her dog in the woods at Hastings.

'I met this woman who was also walking a dog and she told me her daughter was in hospital having her varicose veins done and she had come down from Cambridge to look after the dog. She was a friendly person and we somehow got around to talking about television and a programme the night before about a woman troubled by a ghost who feared she would have to move because of it.

She said, "That's funny, because my other daughter had one."'

'Apparently all manner of things had happened at this daughter's house. When she hung her towels up on a five-angled peg they would be pulled off; taps would be turned off when she was running hot water, and various other things happened in the kitchen. An unseen hand jogged her arm to stop her turning taps on, and if she went out to the kitchen to make an evening drink and put the light on "something" would turn it off again. At first her daughter had laughed about it but in the end it got to them. She and her husband made enquiries and found out from somebody who had lived in the neighbourhood many years ago that the ground on which the estate was built had belonged to a farmer who had eleven children. They were a terrible crowd, used to do diabolical things; there was no parental control at all and they were often in trouble with the police. It was thought that if one of this brood had died it could be their spirit responsible for the upsets, because it was definitely a mischievous spirit and not an evil one. However, it was enough to be very annoying and in the end they decided to move.'

Lastly, a haunted school. There must be a statistic about the number of small boys who hated their prep school; quite a number of them, in my experience. Few ever got their own back for those dismal early schooldays, but I know of one boy who did, and in the most satisfying way.

Young Norman, sent to a prep school in Battle, Sussex, found the headmaster's wife to be a veritable monster. She went about in slippers, creeping up on the boys, who would never hear her coming. She was always sneaking around to see if they were up to something. She would listen at doors and suddenly walk in. When she caught a miscreant, heaven help him; a caning from her husband resulted. She made life a perfect misery.

Many years later the school became a girls' school. Grown-up Norman now had schoolgirl daughters of his own and he was astonished when they told him they had met girls who had been at his former prep school and that it was haunted. The apparition had been seen several times, just half a ghost, the upper half, but plainly visible. From their description Norman recognised the ghost at once. It was the headmaster's wife.

Norman (now a respected professor) told me: 'I had a picture in my mind, from what my daughters were telling me, of her standing in the corridor at the east end of the school, where some of the dormitories were. I was surprised in one way but not in another. If anyone was glued to this planet and didn't take off to heaven it would be that woman, in my opinion. I couldn't bear her.'

The Town of Eight Hundred Ghosts

Britain has more ghosts than any other country in the world. Yet it was not until the late Victorian years that anyone got around to compiling some reliable ghostly statistics.

In the 1890s an extensive survey called the Census of Hallucinations interviewed seventeen thousand people and revealed how many of them claimed to have had a ghostly encounter. The question put to them was: 'Have you ever, when believing yourself to be completely awake, seen or been touched by a living being; which impression, so far as you could discover, was not due to any external physical cause?'

Almost one person in ten answered yes.

This figure of one in ten people having a ghostly encounter is worth remembering, for, as you will see, it has remained remarkably consistent.

The Census, an early pioneer among polls, was informative in other ways. It revealed that only a minority of ghosts seemed to haunt the living for a purpose, such as to point out hidden caches of money with which debts could be paid. The majority of ghosts showed 'an absence of any apparent intelligent action ... If their visits have an objective, they certainly fail to reveal it.'

The Census also presented ample evidence of the by no means uncommon phenomenon of ghosts appearing to family and friends at or after death.

Half a century later, soon after the Second World War, a national newspaper, the *Daily Herald*, published the results of a country-wide poll. This found that more than one in three people believed in ghosts, and that women had a far greater belief in the supernatural than men.

Out of all those questioned, only one person in a hundred rejected any manifestations of the supernatural.

The pollsters reported that very often a logical refusal to believe in ghosts was coupled with an emotional fear. A housewife said, for instance, 'I don't believe in ghosts in the daytime – only at night.' While another remarked, 'I'll believe in one when I see one, but please God don't send me one to prove it!'

In the 1950s another poll, conducted for another national newspaper, the *News Chronicle*, and covering 'a representative section of men and women in all walks of life in England, Scotland and Wales', produced the fact that one person in ten believed in ghosts. And again, that more women than men were found to believe in them.

There were three characteristics of the answers given in this poll which were particularly illuminating. These were:

Young people were more inclined to believe in ghosts than their elders;

A greater belief was found among prosperous sections of the community than among poorer people;

And the more educated people were, the greater was the chance that they would say yes.

An added finding of this poll was that two out of every ten people who admitted to a belief in ghosts had actually seen one.

In the 1960s the intriguing information was published that there were more than ten thousand haunted premises in the British Isles, a figure arrived at from records of the British Travel Association and other sources.

The new openness about ghosts, with more people admitting to seeing them instead of keeping quiet for fear of ridicule, now stretched to the property market. From the Cotswolds to Cornwall there was an unusual surge of activity, as houseowners and estate agents discovered that a ghost on the premises, far from being a disadvantage, could put pounds on a purchase. Ghosts started to be mentioned in property descriptions.

Some agents reported a waiting list of clients wanting old houses with ghosts attached. In Devon, during this curious boom, some owners of reputedly haunted dilapidated old manor houses started asking such ridiculous prices that in some cases it meant the ghost cost more than the property.

The majority of people seeking a property with a ghost were usually found to be middle-aged and without children. They were generally people who had no particular interest in the supernatural but just fancied having a (harmless, and preferably well-authenticated) ghost about the house.

The ghosts offered in these instances ranged from spectral historical figures to an unknown man in red, a ghostly dog that panted loudly, and a spirit that was always busily moving things about in the bathroom. One hopes that the people who acquired these properties considered they had their money's worth.

In the aftermath of this activity in the property market came a new set of ghostly statistics from a most unlikely source. Not, this time, from a nationwide poll, but from a single small town in the Midlands.

'Dawley, Shropshire. Grey houses packed side by side among grassy mounds that used to be the spoil heaps of the pits that made the town's name as the home of Victorian ironmasters. The old buildings wait for the sprawl of

Telford New Town, three miles away, to take them over and bring life again.'

Such was an outsider's view of Dawley in 1970. A town whose population of eight thousand remained the same as before the Second World War. Indeed, a town most people had never heard of.

All that changed as Dawley shot to national fame overnight.

It all came about as a result of research by Geoffrey Nelson, of Birmingham Polytechnic, and Rosemary Clews, of the University of Birmingham. The two conducted a serious survey of religious beliefs and behaviour in Dawley. Out of the meticulous facts and figures of their sociological study came the surprise revelation that no fewer than one-tenth of the inhabitants of Dawley claimed to have seen or felt the presence of a ghost. Even people who said they did not believe in ghosts claimed to have seen them.

When these findings were reported at a British Association conference, Dawley became instantly famous as 'the town with eight hundred haunted people'. And hotfoot on the ghost trail came the newspaper reporters and other interested parties.

Much as the two researchers tried to explain that their scholastic survey had sought to establish patterns of religious behaviour in the area, such as who went to church, who didn't, and why, and that the question about ghosts was only a subsidiary one, the newspaper sleuths were out for what they could find, and they did turn up quite a bit. What made this survey so intriguing was that it had been conducted among a down-to-earth people stated to be 'hard-headed, hard-hearted and hard-bitten, believing in nothing they can't see or sit on'.

It was suggested that ministers in Dawley in the last century had preached hellfire to the people and it had put all kinds of fears into their minds; that they may have iron in their hearts and souls from the days of the great ironmasters, but beneath it all they were still country folk; that down at the old folk's centre any afternoon the hymn singing was just like a revivalist meeting. The old fear of hellfire, the old superstitions, were still rife. People still talked of the pit disaster when nine miners ignored pulpit warnings against working on Sundays. The slings used to lower them into the shaft broke and they plunged to their deaths. It was a judgement, some said and, they claimed, the miners' ghosts still walked.

There were other traditional ghosts like Barney, the Jewish pedlar, murdered at a stile eighty years ago, who walked the field where he died. But there were other, current hauntings, even in the local vicarage, where a ghost without a name made noises in the night; both the vicar and his wife had heard them. Over at The Swan, an old coaching house on Watling Street, they were troubled by a ghost who walked the bedrooms. They called him Humphrey. He was quite harmless and had a sense of humour, the landlord said. He and his wife heard Humphrey's footsteps plain as could be; sometimes they sounded all round the inn, rousing the dogs. Humphrey also liked to move pictures around on the wall, slipping them from their nails, and so on. The landlord and his wife had never actually seen Humphrey, but the cook had. She saw him striding along the landing. He wore a long coat and trousers of untanned leather.

Then there were the individual cases discovered among the townsfolk, people of all ages. There was the young girl who, passing the church at Ironbridge at midnight, saw ghostly figures dressed in white. She ran for her life. There was the middle-aged lady who saw ghosts often: the ghosts of her husband, who had died three years ago, and of her mother and father. Her husband had told her not to worry, that she'd be all right. There was even, shades of that hellfire, the man in his forties who had had a dreadful fright when he was a lad. He was walking home from Oakengate Fair when he suddenly saw 'this thing' in the road in front of him. It had a great head and horns and there were flames coming out of its mouth.

So the evidence was there right enough. Satisfied, the reporters and the curious retreated, and Dawley dropped back into obscurity. But the hard statistic remained: one person in ten had experienced a ghost. And so it was confirmed only a few years later, when the Census of Hallucinations of 1894 was repeated on a much smaller scale in 1977, with only eight hundred people being interviewed. Once more, almost one in ten reported personal experience of having seen or having been touched by a ghost. Over eighty years on, and the findings were exactly the same.

There is an additional statistic which I would like to present to you. It is this: one person in eight has either experienced a haunting, or knows someone who has, or has first-hand knowledge of one.

You don't have to take my word for it; this is a statistic you can prove for yourself. Ask around among family, friends and acquaintances.

I was once interviewed on the phone by an editor of women's magazines. We got on famously until I mentioned that statistic: one in eight. 'Oh, there's nothing like that in my family,' she said, and I felt the beginnings of scepticism creeping in. Then she suddenly remembered. 'Oh, yes, I did have an uncle who offered £100 to anyone who would sleep in a certain room in his house ...'

So you see, it does work. Try it yourself.

Strange Sounds of War

It was a black day in the Second World War. On 19 August 1942, an Anglo-Canadian force raided the heavily defended Channel port of Dieppe, in Hitler's 'Fortress Europe'. The ill-conceived, inadequately supported operation was a disastrous and bloody failure. More than two-thirds of the five thousand Canadian troops who took part in the assault were killed, wounded or captured.

Ten years later and seven years after the end of the war, the tragedy of the Dieppe raid had receded into history. Certainly the two young women who went for a holiday near Dieppe in August 1952 had given little thought to its bleak wartime role. They had read in the newspapers years ago about the Dieppe raid, but no more than that. Neither of them had looked up any history about it.

Which made all the more strange what followed.

The women were Mrs Dorothy Norton, aged thirty-two, accompanied by her two young children, and her sister-in-law, Miss Agnes Norton. The two shared a bedroom on the second floor of a three-storey house facing the sea, which was about a quarter of a mile away down a steep path. They were told the house had been used as quarters for German troops during the war. The two children, who at no time heard anything unusual, were on the same floor, but were in a bedroom two doors away.

Both women's wristwatches were set to single summertime, one hour ahead of GMT. This time was also in use during the Dieppe raid.

And this is what Mrs Dorothy Norton told psychic investigators:

'At 4.20 a.m. on Saturday, 4 August, Agnes got up and went out of the room. She came back in a few minutes and said: "Do you hear that noise?"

'I had, in fact, been listening to it for about twenty minutes. It started suddenly and sounded like a storm at sea. Agnes said she had also been listening to it for about twenty minutes. We lay in the dark listening to the sound.

'We could distinctly hear cries and shouts and gunfire. When we put on the light it still continued. We went out on the balcony where we could look towards the beach, although we could not see it. We heard the sound of guns and dive-bombing distinctly, many times. Then came the sound of shells.

'At 4.50 it suddenly stopped. At 5.05 a.m. it started again and became so loud that as we stood on our balcony we were amazed it did not wake other people in the house.

'By now it was getting light. The cocks were crowing, the birds singing. We heard a rifle shot on the hill above the beach. Then we heard dive-bombers and cries and shouts.

'The noise, which was very loud, stopped abruptly at 5.40. At 5.50 it started again, not so loudly, and sounded more like aeroplanes. At 6.20 the sound came again but fainter. Then I fell asleep as the experience had made me very tired.

'I was woken by a similar sound on the following Monday, only fainter. At the end of it I seemed to hear a lot of men singing. When the cocks started crowing I went back to sleep. On this occasion my sister-in-law did not awaken.'

What the two women mysteriously heard can be compared with what actually happened on the day of the

Dieppe raid ten years before. This is the official report:

> 3.47 a.m. Approaching assault vessels ran across a German convoy. Firing which began immediately went on until after 4 a.m. Near Dieppe, there was shouting by German soldiers manning the beach defences.
>
> 4.50 a.m. Zero hour for some of the landings. There may have been silence at this stage.
>
> 5.07 a.m. First wave of landing craft touched down in the face of heavy fire.
>
> 5.12 a.m. Destroyers began to bombard Dieppe.
>
> 5.15 a.m. Low-flying Hurricanes attacked the sea front buildings.
>
> 5.20 a.m. Main Dieppe force began to land in the face of heavy fire.
>
> 5.40 a.m. Naval bombardment ceased.
>
> 5.50 a.m. Forty-eight RAF aircraft arrived from England.

Mrs Dorothy Norton's bizarre testimony of the ghost noises she and her sister-in-law heard remains on the files of the Society for Psychical Research. Investigators decided that it would be rash to assume that the sounds heard by the two women were a sort of ghostly soundtrack repetition of the raid as there was not enough detailed information as to when the several kinds of sound appeared to judge whether they did take place at exactly the same time. But that Dorothy and Agnes Norton had heard what they heard was beyond question.

Still on the subject of ghostly wartime 'replays' is this experience of Mary Punchard, of Southsea, Hants.

'I saw a vision at Beachy Head, Sussex, at the end of the war. I did not know of the existence of the barbed wire at that place till I actually got there for my first walk after the war.

'Then I saw scattered around me the remains of a burnt-out Spitfire. Tears began to pour down my face as I picked up scraps of forage caps, shirt collars and especially the eyelets of burnt-to-a-cinder boots.

'The person I was with saw nothing. But I saw six or seven airmen standing around chatting in groups and smoking and looking somewhat bewildered. I saw them as plainly as I saw my companion – but he saw no one.

'It was as though those men were crying out within me: "Oh, the hopelessness of it all, oh, the futility of war!"'

Finally, on ghostly noises, this eerie experience of Tom Sankey, of Sedgley, Worcestershire, must be among the strangest.

'My father was in charge of a public swimming baths near Liverpool. On Sunday mornings, when the place was closed, we would often go in for a swim.

'Once while we were sitting there we became aware that the intense silence of the building was welling into sound. Fascinated, we held our breath and listened. Quite suddenly, and all around us, the sounds grew, as if someone was turning up a hidden volume control. We heard the shouts and screams and splashes of people, just as if the pool was crowded.

'Every Sunday we would stand listening morbidly to what I described as the "death cries of all those drowned in the bath during the previous week". If only we could have looked ahead to the night of 6 May 1941. Then we learned the horrifying prophetic truth of it all.

'This was the time of the heavy German air-raid Blitz which struck so savagely at Liverpool and Bootle. The swimming baths had been boarded over and the building was being used as a mortuary.

'There were nearly three hundred bodies laid out in the building. At the height of the evening raid a timber yard behind the baths was ignited. The whole block was soon soaring in flames. When the raid was over we came out and stood silently watching the crackling fires.

'Nearly three hundred corpses lay where the swimming baths had once been. It had well and truly become the "House of Death" after all.'

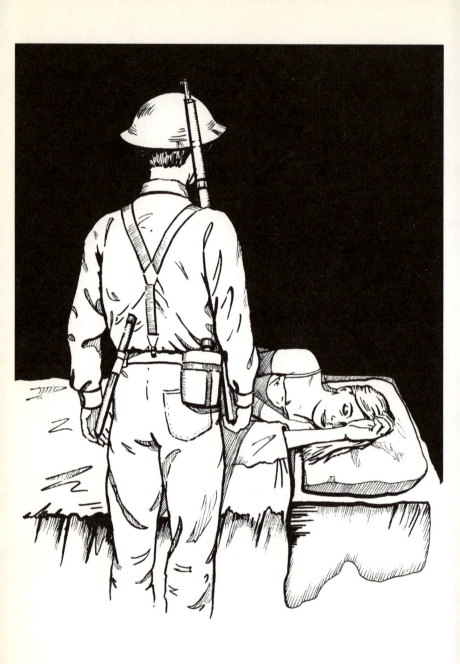

And They Came Back

Young Birmingham girl Ethel Meeson was very close to her older brother, Bert. He doted on her, at nine years old the baby of the family. 'Bab' he lovingly called her.

When the First World War broke out Bert volunteered for the Hussars, and Ethel was so proud of him when he came home on leave in his scarlet uniform with a cockade in his hat. Sadly, Bert took part in one of the first cavalry charges of the war and was killed instantly.

The tragic news had not yet reached the family when little Ethel, asleep in bed one night, awoke suddenly to see Bert in his uniform standing at the foot of the bed. He told her, 'Don't worry about me, Bab, I'm all right.'

When the War Office telegram was delivered some time later Ethel realised that it was on the very night of his death that Bert had come to her.

Ethel told of this very real incident all her life. How do I know the story? Ethel was my mother-in-law.

Our friend Mrs Joan Thwaites' father died a few years ago. She was the eldest daughter and they had been particularly close. After the funeral she felt very bad about 'leaving my Dad in the cold when we had all come back into the warm, laughing and talking'.

One stormy night a few weeks later she woke up to see her father standing by the bed. 'Don't worry about me, Joan,' he said, 'I'm all right.' She never had that bad feeling again.

Two isolated incidents? No, two very common occurrences, and there is overwhelming evidence to prove it.

Most recently in 1994, a senior clinical psychiatrist did not mince words when he told a conference of the Society for Scientific Exploration, in Glasgow, that reports of ghostly apparitions could not be dismissed as the 'rantings of the insane or the work of hoaxers'. Professor Ian Stevenson, who had studied reports of ghosts in Britain and the United States, said the people to whom the dead appeared had normal, healthy minds. There appeared to be an explanation for the sightings which defied traditional science. He had studied cases dating back forty years in which someone who had died or was about to die appeared to a close friend, and these reports could be checked by scrutinising death certificates and by carefully controlled interviews with the person and family involved. Studies with the mentally ill had clearly shown that they were not gifted to see such apparitions.

These worthy findings confirm what countless ordinary families already know and many people have experienced. It is perfectly normal to see apparitions of loved ones and friends at or after death.

Here are two cases that show how even extreme distance is no bar to a ghostly appearance at death. They are separated by a hundred years, yet show a remarkable consistency.

The first incident, which comes from the 1890s, concerns the well-documented case of Mr Walker-Anderson, a Yorkshireman who had emigrated to Australia. He described how he awoke on the evening of

17 November 1891, to see the figure of his aunt, 'Mrs P.', standing near the foot of the bed, looking older and stouter than when he had last seen her three years earlier. Her lips moved, although he heard no sounds, and he seemed to catch that she meant 'Goodbye'. The following morning Mr Walker-Anderson told his wife of the apparition he had seen and wrote down on a piece of paper, 'I believe Aunt P. died on the 17th November', and put it in a drawer.

In due course the English newspapers for that week arrived by boat and sure enough, there was a death notice of his Aunt P., who had indeed died on that date. Subsequent correspondence with his mother revealed that, taking into account the time difference between Melbourne and Greenwich, Aunt P. had appeared to her nephew in Australia three hours after her death in England.

Now on to the 1990s and this account of our second case from my friend Joy Clark.

'Evelyn was a shorthand typist in the office where I worked in Caterham, Surrey. She was a lovely young woman and I liked her; when we all had to make things for a bring-and-buy or some "do" we were having at the office she made the most wonderful French croissants! She had a daughter aged about twelve and an older son who was over in the United States studying law.

'One day she came in very excited to tell me that she and her husband and daughter were going for a holiday in the States to visit their son. The only problem was that she had her elderly mother living with her and the old lady did not take kindly to having to go and stay with her son (Evelyn's brother) while Evelyn was away. However, she did finally agree to go, so everything was settled.

'Their holiday went splendidly as planned, and after spending some time with their son Evelyn and her husband hired a car and drove up into the mountains with their daughter. It was a very mountainous region and the view was magnificent. There were two roads up the mountains and they chose to follow the one that was not so close to the edge. After a while they pulled into a lonely spot to have their picnic. As they were sitting there her daughter, turning round in the car and looking out the back, said, "Oh, there's an old lady come out". They thought this very strange as they were really quite high in the mountains and had seen no signs of life anywhere, and certainly no living accommodation. They sat in the car almost waiting for the woman to walk past, an elderly woman wearing a black shawl with a black scarf over her head. The daughter had wound down her window at the back, and as the woman drew level with the car she looked right in. The daughter screamed and cried, "Mummy, Mummy, it's Grandma!" Evelyn turned round and, as she later told me, looked straight into her mother's face. Her husband had started the car but it had only gone a few yards when she told him to stop – "You must stop, it's my mother, I know it's my mother!" But when they got out of the car there was no one there.

'The husband couldn't believe what had happened but, with the daughter very upset and Evelyn shocked and in tears, their outing was ruined. They drove back to the hotel where they were staying. Evelyn asked the manager if there had been any messages and he said yes, her brother had telephoned from England and asked if she would phone back after a certain time to allow for the several hours' difference. This she did, and her worst fears were confirmed when he told her that her mother had died. She had passed away in her armchair at almost the same time that Evelyn and her daughter had seen her look into the car. By then all Evelyn wanted to know was, what was her mother wearing at the time? Her brother was indignant at being asked such a trivial question, but then he told her: Mother had been wearing her black shawl. She had others in different colours, but that day she had chosen the black one.

'Evelyn repeated this story to me several times (I used to give her lifts) and she said, "It was my mother, you know, Joy. Does anyone mistake their own mother's face? It was my mother, she had come to say goodbye to us."

Needless to say, their holiday was cut short and they came home.

Reappearances can take many forms, sometimes occurring long afterwards, as with our friend Vera Bolton in the Midlands.

'I had been reading in bed one night for quite a long time. Eventually I put the book down and composed myself for sleep. After lying awake for a considerable time, I heard footsteps going towards the bathroom from the adjoining bedroom. I then heard the footsteps return from the bathroom and go downstairs. I assumed it was my husband, probably fetching a drink of water. The footsteps returned again after a short interval and appeared to return to the adjoining bedroom.

'I lay for a long time expecting my husband to pop his head round the door to see if I was awake. Then the realisation came to me, how could it have been him – he had been dead for seven years! Nevertheless, I decided to get up and find out what was going on. At first reluctant to put the light on, but clutching my Lifeline pendant in my tightly clenched hand, I went from room to room, listening for sounds, but saw and heard nothing. I then returned to my bedroom completely mystified, because I was convinced I had not been dreaming.'

Many bereaved people continue to sense, see and hear the physical presence of loved ones for long periods. Again, this is perfectly normal and the experiences very real.

My friend Olive Keell lives alone but is never lonely. For, six months after her husband died, he came back, and he has been around the house, in Sussex, ever since.

Olive and Cyril enjoyed eighteen years of happy marriage after long years of waiting for each other. When, after death, he suddenly returned to her in the middle of the night she was surprised but not shocked.

'When I awoke to see him there I thought at first it was a dream, but then it became clear that I was awake and he was real, so real that I spoke to him, but when I did so he quickly faded away. After that he began to appear quite regularly. I still very much wanted to speak to him but I learned not to do so, for then he would remain for several seconds and not vanish immediately.'

Olive is in her seventies, a very down-to-earth person, as becomes a lifetime in nursing. She is also an outgoing lady and a wonderful cook, whose generous output and quality of cakes and dishes for local charity events is legendary.

She told me that when her husband was alive she sometimes used to get up in the middle of the night and do things because she couldn't sleep. She would then hear Cyril's footsteps and him calling, 'Give over, dear, and come back to bed'. Often now, on getting up in the night, she hears his footsteps along the hall and hears his voice in her head calling her back to bed, just as he used to.

On his frequent visits Cyril often appears in the hall, usually wearing a favourite greeny-grey cardigan and slacks and with his walking stick. He'll stand and smile at her before turning as he disappears. Olive finds it very comforting to see him; it makes her feel that he is thinking about her, just as she thinks of him.

A newer development of Cyril's visitations came when he also began to appear as a shadow. As Olive came out of the kitchen one day with the light behind her, her shadow was cast in front of her together with another shadow. She stopped in surprise and went back into the kitchen to see if anyone was there. There was not, but as she left the kitchen again the same thing happened. It could only be

Cyril, literally shadowing her. Then, the other day there was a whisk of something quick at the end of the passage. 'For heaven's sake,' she exclaimed, 'stay still for a moment, Cyril!'

No, Olive is never lonely.

The curious experience of widowed Mrs Maureen Burt did not involve an apparition but something very different and quite inexplicable.

Her husband was a scaffolder. Because of the dangerous nature of his job he used to keep his wristwatch, a digital one, in a tin, wrapped in a handkerchief, in his pocket. When he fell sick and did not go to work for some time the tin was put away in a drawer. The watch battery had pretty well worn out anyway, so he did not take it to work again. Then he died.

The next night at eleven o'clock Maureen heard this little ringing sound. She searched the house, then realised it was coming from the drawer. She opened it, opened the tin and found the alarm going on her late husband's watch. She thought it strange but switched it off and put it back in the tin in the drawer.

The following night at eleven o'clock her sixteen-year-old son was with her when the watch alarm went off again. 'Oh, I put that off last night,' she said. This time her son got the watch out and told her, 'You couldn't have done.' He switched it to the off position again. 'I thought the battery had worn out,' he said, putting it back in the drawer.

The third night the watch rang again at eleven o'clock. This time the son was uneasy. He took the battery out and threw it up the garden. 'That will stop it,' he said firmly, putting the watch back in the drawer.

But the next night the alarm went off again at eleven o'clock, although there was no battery in the watch. That was the end of it, though; it never sounded again.

Now to a story which takes us back to the First World War, but one which is highly unusual to say the least.

Young Mary Ellen Balchin's husband was among the first soldiers to go over to France on the outbreak of war in 1914. Sergeant Leonard Balchin of the Royal North Lancs regiment was a member of what the Kaiser scornfully described as Britain's 'contemptible little army'.

One night Mary Ellen awoke at her home in Crayford, Kent, to see her husband standing at the foot of the bed. He was dressed in his uniform, just as she had seen him before he went away. And he spoke to her. 'I'm all right,' he told her lovingly, 'don't worry.' He then faded from view.

Mary Ellen did not know what to make of her husband's sudden ghostly appearance, but the very next day she received a telegram from the War Office informing her that he had been killed in action.

After her strange experience of the night before, she refused to believe it. 'No,' she stoutly told everyone, 'Leonard's all right, he told me so and not to worry.'

Her faith was not misplaced. Sergeant Balchin was found three days later in No Man's Land, severely wounded. German fighter planes strafed the Red Cross convoy taking him back behind the lines. 'They couldn't get me the first time, so the buggers tried again!' he joked. He was wounded twice more but survived that devastating war, being commissioned in the field after all his officers were killed.

Leonard Balchin ended the war as a captain and lived on to the grand age of eighty-eight. His wife, all her life, never forgot the vividness of his ghostly visitation to her that night, as he lay critically wounded on the battlefield.

My informant for this extraordinary story? Mary Ellen's daughter, Barbara.

The Mystic Healing Hand

Anyone opening their daily newspaper one summer's morning in 1995 and seeing the story it contained, would have been excused for thinking they had suddenly slipped back a century. That is, unless they held the profound belief that many do. For there, in black and white, was the surprising story of a priest who had been brought back from the brink of death by the mystic powers of a 300-year-old healing hand.

The news reports said that doctors at Hereford County Hospital had pronounced that Father Christopher Jenkins, a Benedictine monk in his sixties who suffered a severe stroke, had regrettably little or no chance of recovery. He lay in a dying coma.

But a colleague, Father Anthony Tumelty, took the healing 'Kemble Hand' from its place on the altar at St Francis Xavier Church, Hereford, to Father Jenkins's bedside. He removed the relic from its oak casket and placed it on the sick man's head. From that time, he began to recover.

Nobody had expected Father Jenkins to live, but he came out of the coma within hours and in a day or two was walking, talking and eating – to the great surprise of the doctors.

It was the latest in a long list of miraculous recoveries attributed to the Kemble Hand and its ghostly properties.

In 1990 Canon William O'Connor, of Cork, in the Republic of Ireland, was dying from a blood disorder, but recovered when a friend flew the hand to his bedside.

The hand's possessor, Father John Kemble, was a seventeenth-century Catholic priest who was active in Herefordshire for many years. He led a full, exemplary life and was held in much esteem. But in his seventy-ninth year fate struck. In 1678 he was seized at Pembridge Castle, Herefordshire, where he was chaplain to the Scudamore family. The following year he was tried at Hereford, convicted of having said Mass at Pembridge and sentenced to be hanged, drawn and quartered.

When the under-sheriff came to take him to his execution on Widemarsh Common (22 August 1679) the priest, now eighty years old, asked for time to pray, to smoke a last pipe, and take a last drink. Together the two men shared a cup of wine and a pipe. The hangman also venerated the courageous priest and showed his respect by making sure he was dead after hanging before carrying out the rest of the sentence.

Father Kemble was buried at Welsh Newton churchyard. Pilgrimages were made to his grave and, it was said, miracles wrought there. Two relics of the priest were saved after the execution. One was the severed hand, which a woman picked up and hid under her apron. The other was a piece of linen dipped in his blood.

The hand survived the centuries and is kept in St Francis Xavier Church. Generations of parishioners have believed that the hand has the power to heal. Parish priests take it with them when they visit the sick. The recovered Father Jenkins, a monk at Belmont Abbey, was himself a parish priest at St Francis Xavier.

Martyred Father Kemble is now St John Kemble, having been canonised by the Pope in 1970 as one of the Forty Martyrs of England and Wales.

There are other cases of human relics with mystical healing

properties. One of the most notable is that of Father Edmund Arrowsmith, another Catholic priest, who was executed some fifty years before Father Kemble.

Arrowsmith was a Lancashireman, born at Haydock in 1585, the son of a yeoman farmer. After his ordination at the Jesuit college at Douay, aged twenty-seven, he became renowned for his fearless and forthright ministry in Lancashire. But he had barely a dozen years of freedom before being arrested as a recusant (one who refused to attend Church of England services) and taken under escort to Lancaster.

Father Arrowsmith ultimately faced his accusers at Lancaster Assizes in 1628, charged with having taken the order of priesthood beyond the seas in disobedience to the King's laws. He was found guilty and ordered to be executed. He was forty-three years old.

The execution took place at Lancaster on 28 August 1628. In accordance with the sentence of the time he was first hanged, then his body cut down, dismembered and quartered. His head was set up on a pole amongst the pinnacles of Lancaster Castle and the quarters hung at four points of the building. But one of the dead man's friends managed to recover a hand severed from the body, in compliance with a request from Arrowsmith, so that he might continue his good works from that relic. The hand was taken secretly to a wealthy man's home. It would eventually find a religious venue, but before that, it figured in a bizarre fraud. This was at Ince Hall, near Wigan, which was built around the time of Arrowsmith's death.

When one of the later owners of Ince Hall lay on his deathbed a lawyer was sent for at the last moment to make his will, but before he reached him the man died. In this dilemma it was determined to try the effect of a 'holy hand' upon the corpse, and the lawyer's clerk was sent for it in haste. The body of the dead man was rubbed with the hand of Arrowsmith and it was asserted that he revived sufficiently to sign his will.

After the funeral a daughter of the deceased produced a will which was not signed, leaving the property to the son and daughter, but the wily lawyer soon produced another will, signed with the power of the holy hand and conveying all the property to himself. The son quarrelled with the lawyer, attacked and wounded him and, thinking the wound fatal, left the country and was never heard of again. The daughter also disappeared, but no one knew how or where.

After many years, a gardener at Ince Hall turned up a skull with his spade, and the fate of the vanished daughter was revealed. When this happened Ince Hall had long been uninhabited, for the murdered daughter's ghost was said to have haunted the dishonest lawyer wherever he went – 'suspended in the air before him'. He was reported to have spent the remainder of his days in Wigan, 'the victim of remorse and despair'.

Ince Hall was largely rebuilt years later, following a disastrous fire, but before this there was a room said to be haunted by the ghost of a young woman, presumably the daughter, her shadowy form also being frequently seen by passers-by to hover over the spot where her remains were buried.

As for the hand of Arrowsmith, it was preserved at Bryn Hall until that old mansion was demolished, when it was removed to Garswood Hall, and then finally found a proper home in the Catholic church of St Oswald, Ashton-in-Makerfield, near Wigan, where it became an object of popular veneration.

The holy hand, no longer misused, was credited with having on a number of occasions exhibited an extraordinary influence, and to have brought about many cures of the sick. These successes were celebrated quietly among the community, except when mentioned by the local newspaper for some novel reason; such as when one Catherine Collins, who was paralysed on one side, obtained special leave from Wigan Workhouse to walk to Makerfield in order to receive the application of the holy hand.

Like Father Kemble, Father Arrowsmith was canonised in 1970 as one of the Forty Martyrs of England and Wales.

The Mermaid of the Mere

It is not often that one walks slap-bang into the middle of a legend, but that is what is believed to have happened to a woman visitor to the historic old town of Rye, East Sussex, in the 1950s.

Rye, once a port but now sitting back high inland, with its cobbled streets and half-timbered houses, seems to breathe legends, and it possesses one of the best. This dates back to the fourteenth century and recounts the fall from grace of one of the monks who inhabited the town then.

A member of the Austin (or Augustinian) Friars, known as Brother Cantator because of his beautiful voice, fell hopelessly in love with a local girl named Amanda. The couple secretly made plans to leave Rye and start a new life together in France, but they were betrayed and caught. Brother Cantator's terrible punishment at the hands of his order was to be walled up alive in his cell.

After his first moans and cries of distress Brother Cantator seemed to collect himself, for his fine voice was heard sweetly yet eerily issuing from his living grave. But as he finally succumbed to his fate his sanity broke and shortly before dying he began to gurgle and gobble like a turkey cock. As for Amanda, she died of a broken heart.

The legend has it that during the past six hundred years Brother Cantator's forlorn ghost has wandered in search of his forbidden love. His insane turkey-cock gobbling was claimed to have been heard by Rye residents right up until the nineteenth century. The town's Turkey Cock Lane was so-called as a result of the phenomenon.

And so to the visitor to the town who walked into the legend. She was a lady from Surrey, a guest at a hotel one day in 1952. She was sitting drinking a cup of tea when she noticed a sad-faced monk in a brown habit standing near the party wall with the house next door. She took him to be another guest. He seemed to be rather poorly and, not wishing to embarrass him, she looked away. When she glanced back moments later the figure had gone. It was only afterwards that she learned the sad story of Brother Cantator, whose ghost she must have seen standing at the partition wall, for the house next door was where Amanda reputedly lived.

There was another sighting reported some twenty years later. In 1971 a milkman delivering early one morning in Turkey Cock Lane saw the figure of a monk in full robes at the end of the road. Brother Cantator again?

Other spectral monks figure in haunting legends in Rye. A pawnshop in an old timbered house was haunted for weeks by a yellow-faced monk. Years later, human bones were discovered under a staircase. They were reburied in the churchyard. In the 1930s another monk appeared to the cook of a house in Watchbell Street. This ghost, who followed her into the kitchen, was able to communicate. He said he had been murdered while on a mission from Canterbury and buried in the garden of the house; he was anxious that his remains be found and taken to consecrated ground. However, rather than dig up the whole garden in search of the bones, it was blessed by a priest, which seemed to give release to the restless spirit.

But it is Brother Cantator whose woeful story takes precedence in haunted Rye. Just to walk along Turkey Cock Lane on a summer's afternoon can set the imagination racing.

There is another Rye legend which has stark evidence

to substantiate it. Hanging in the town hall is the gruesome gibbet cage and skull of the murderer Butcher Breeds, who was hanged in 1743 on Gibbets Marsh. This is his story.

Breeds held a grudge against the Mayor of Rye, one James Lamb, who was also a magistrate and had fined Breeds for giving short weight. Breeds determined to get his revenge. One night he lay in wait for Mayor Lamb on the pathway in the churchyard at midnight and pounced as soon as that worthy appeared. However, in the darkness he mistakenly stabbed and killed Lamb's brother-in-law, Alan Grebell, who had unfortunately borrowed the Mayor's cloak that night. Breeds was eventually arrested after dancing drunkenly through the streets shouting, 'Butchers kill lambs!'

The skull is all that remains of Breeds, the rest of his bones were stolen; it was believed they would cure rheumatism if used in a soup. But the ghosts of Butcher Breeds and Alan Grebell are said to haunt the churchyard to this day.

It seems hardly surprising in this atmosphere that one of the scariest ghost stories in the English language was written in Rye. For it was here, at Lamb House in 1898, that Henry James wrote *The Turn of the Screw*. The memorable 1961 film of this story, called *The Innocents*, starred Deborah Kerr as the young governess of two orphaned children who begins to see strange, ghostly figures whose descriptions match those of the house's former valet and governess. And the intruders are looking for the children ...

Many believe James drew on haunted Rye for his fictional 'Bly'. And two other famous literary residents of Lamb House (now with the National Trust), Rumer Godden and E.F. Benson, claimed to have heard eerie children's voices there when there were no children.

Now to a town built on a legend. Bungay, in Suffolk, is the accredited home of the fearsome Black Dog. The evidence of this devilish creature comes to us across the years from the Rev. Abraham Fleming, who wrote a vivid account of it at the time. In a pamphlet he relates the 'Straunge and Terrible Wunder' of how, in the midst of a severe thunderstorm in 1577, St Mary's Church in Bungay was plunged into darkness. Then a flaming black dog, or 'the divel in such a likeness', appeared 'running all along the body of the church with great swiftnesse, and incredible haste'. The animal seized upon two people praying for mercy and 'as it seemed, wrung the necks of them bothe at one instant clene backward'. The dog then jumped on another man and 'gave him such a gripe on the back, that therewith all he was presently drawen togither and shrunk up, as it were a peece of lether scorched in a hot fire'. Miraculously, the cleric says, this man survived.

In the four hundred years since, the Black Dog is said to have been sighted in Bungay on many occasions. It is thought to be associated with Black Shuck, a spectral devil dog that haunts the East Anglia region. It is usually seen at night, and a meeting with it is said to be an omen of disaster.

Despite its sinister nature, however, the hellhound of Bungay has become an unofficial emblem of the town, being perpetuated in some unlikely ways. There is, for instance, a Black Dog football team, a Black Dog Running Club, and a Black Dog Marathon; while local business also makes use of the 'brand' name. An evocative image of the devil dog, teeth bared, leaps forward on a zigzag of lightning on the town's weathervane. So far so good, but in the closing years of the 1990s an idea to celebrate the millennium by erecting a bronze statue of the beast in the town centre met its critics. The main objection was that the Black Dog was a nasty, evil creature clearly in league with the devil; it was hardly a suitable candidate for such a momentous occasion. But the people of Bungay in general love their demon hound and take a proprietorial view of it. As one of the many supporters of the idea said, 'After all, our Black Dog *is* only a legend. Isn't it?'

There are many legends of baleful forces killing off owners of English stately homes, but the tale of Chavenage must rank with the best of them. The dark force at this Elizabethan manor near Tetbury, Gloucestershire, allegedly accounted for the extinction of an entire family.

The remarkable chain of events began during the English Civil War. The manor was owned at that time by Nathaniel Stephens, a Member of Parliament who raised a regiment of horse in support of Oliver Cromwell. Although a moderate, he was persuaded by Cromwell's son-in-law, General Henry Ireton (to whom Stephens was also related by marriage), to agree to Charles I's execution in 1649.

Stephens's daughter, Abigail, horrified and furious at what her father had done, cursed him. He fell mortally ill and, as the neighbouring gentry gathered for his funeral, a hearse drew up at the door driven by a headless man. Stephens was seen to rise from his coffin and enter the hearse, whereupon the headless driver assumed the appearance of the martyred King Charles and the carriage galloped away, disappearing amid flames at the gates of the park.

The same grim hearse, the story goes, came back to carry off all male Stephens heirs from their deathbed until the line died out in the nineteenth century.

Some rooms at Chavenage have remained haunted to this day. Guests put into either of the adjoining rooms in which Cromwell and Ireton once stayed, have woken in a cold sweat, filled with terror. Whether the shades of Ireton and his father-in-law the Lord Protector have any responsibility for that is open to question; for at the Restoration the bodies of both men were disinterred from their graves and hanged at Tyburn in a show of public wrath.

However, Princess Marie-Louise, Queen Victoria's grand-daughter, certainly felt a malign presence outside those rooms, while guests in other rooms have each had the same dream of a black-whiskered man wearing epaulettes bending over their bed. Then there is the visiting clergyman who found himself praying with a ghostly monk in the chapel.

The ghosts have remained at Chavenage in spite of efforts by clergy to send them on their way; all part of the attraction for visitors to this mellow old manor which is often used as a location for films and television.

The sound of ghostly bagpipes pervades many a Scottish legend, but I think the story of the brave Piper of Duntroon is one on its own.

Duntroon Castle, on the shore of Loch Crinan on the coast of Argyll, is an ancient fortress of the Campbells. In the early part of the seventeenth century Colla Ciotach, a celebrated general in the army of the Marquess of Montrose, raided the castle and captured it from the Campbells. He left a MacDonald garrison there and sailed with his men across the sea to the Hebridean island of Islay, then a MacDonald stronghold. But during his absence the Campbells returned to Duntroon in force, overpowered the garrison and again occupied the castle. The garrison were killed or taken prisoner, but the piper, always a privileged person in those days, was allowed a measure of liberty.

As the days went by, the lonely piper was filled with apprehension at the thought of Colla Ciotach unwittingly returning to the castle not knowing of the change of hands, and sure enough that is what did happen. One morning the piper was appalled to see the war galley of his chief entering Loch Crinan, steering unsuspectingly towards the castle. The piper hurried down to the rocky shore and on the spot composed the tune which, through the centuries, has been his memorial. Known as 'The Piper's Warning to his Master', the tune, or pibroch, begged the chief to avoid the castle, telling him that he himself was a prisoner.

Although words to this tune have been handed down, it is said that the great pipers of the time could literally make their pipes speak, and could, therefore, convey, without the spoken word, the sense of urgency or alarm. Certainly on this occasion the warning was understood by Colla Ciotach, who promptly altered course and stood out to sea.

The brave piper was seized, his fingers were cut off, and he received such treatment that he died. He was buried, it was said, under the flagstones of the castle kitchen. For long years afterwards his ghost haunted the castle, the thin notes of ghostly piping being heard after midnight.

There is a sequel to this story. In the 1860s, workmen making alterations to the castle kitchen discovered the skeleton of a man buried there. The remains were given a Christian burial, since when the piper's ghost has no longer been seen nor his ghostly music heard.

At another Scottish castle a ghost still walks, though this has nothing to do with the pipes or ancient wars. The ghost here is that of a sad young lady.

Comlongon Castle in Dumfriesshire, a fifteenth-century keep on the Solway coast, has been transformed into a popular hotel, but the ghost apparently lingers on, four hundred years after her untimely death. She was Lady Marion Carruthers, a young girl who knew her own mind. She had sought sanctuary at Comlongon from her uncle, Sir Charles Murray, and an unwanted marriage to the nephew of the Duke of Drumlanrig, one John McMath. Unfortunately for Marion the engagement was granted a royal blessing, and an order was given to take her from the castle and marry her forcibly to McMath. In her despair, Marion ran to the top of the castle and leapt out of a window, plunging seventy-five feet to a bloody death.

The legend says that grass has never grown on the spot by the east wall where her body landed on that dreadful day in 1564, while Marion herself restlessly paces the castle and its surrounds, accompanied by the sharp smell of apples. And several guests at the hotel are reported to have witnessed strange happenings.

One is left speculating on the patently odious nature of the nephew who drove poor Marion to take such a drastic way out.

The curious case of the widow Thornel is remembered at Shipston-on-Stour, Warwickshire, and with good reason. Her death nearly three hundred years ago brought a tragic sequel in the 1950s.

It was in June 1695 that two farm workers reported seeing a witch flying on a broomstick through an apple orchard. Town officials and clergy who hurried to investigate found no witch but blind Elizabeth Thornel, in her eighties, hanging from a bough. The old woman had long been suspected of dealings with the devil, so her death drew no sympathy. The usual burial procedure for witches was followed and she was lowered into her grave with a stake driven through her heart.

Was the widow Thornel really a witch, and was there, therefore, a curse on anyone who thereafter disturbed her bones?

On 20 July 1951 workmen laying a new sewer in West Street came upon fragments of human bone at the exact spot where Elizabeth Thornel had been buried so long ago. No mention was made of the find, however, when the trench collapsed and killed a workman a short time later. It was considered the grim facts would upset the dead man's family.

The story of the old Mint House at Pevensey, Sussex, comes from Elizabethan times and is a particularly grisly one. The timber-framed house, built on the site of a Norman mint, was rented at the time by Thomas Dight, a London merchant. One day Dight, apparently a man of a very jealous nature, returned home unexpectedly to find his wife with her lover. The unfortunate woman was tied up, her tongue was cut out, and she was forced to witness her lover being slowly roasted to death over a fire. Dight then disposed of the body into the sea, locked his wife in a room and left her to die. His heinous double crime only came to light some fifteen years later, when he made a full confession on his deathbed.

Over the years there have been many sightings of a ghostly woman in the Mint House and instances of visitors feeling or sensing a creepy presence there.

Of all the many haunting legends, my favourite has to be that of Rostherne Mere, in Cheshire. The mere, near Knutsford, is believed to be just a fragment of the original lake that once existed in the area. In recent times it has measured nearly two-thirds of a mile, covering some one hundred and eighteen acres, but that is said to be only a tenth of the size it used to be, a vast expanse of water covering all the ground lying between Alderley Edge and High Legh. It was at one time thought to be bottomless. During the nineteenth century, however, an intrepid Captain Cotton proved, by means of soundings, that it was in fact some seventeen fathoms, or one hundred and two feet deep. That is still twice as deep as many parts of the North Sea.

And now to the fascinating legend attached to Rostherne Mere, which tells of a mermaid who invariably appeared there at dawn on Easter Sunday. The mere was not her home. This was reputed to be somewhere along the banks of the River Mersey, away in the direction of Liverpool. Many claimed that there was a secret subterranean tunnel linking the Mersey and the mere, through which the bewitching creature swam.

Until well into the nineteenth century there were people who believed in the mermaid's existence. On Easter Sunday morning there was an annual pilgrimage to the side of the mere by people anxious to catch a glimpse of this beautiful mythical creature. Many people claimed to have heard her ring a church bell which lay submerged in the mere (it had been lost there years earlier on rolling away from workmen trying to hang it in the medieval church). Afterwards, the mermaid's ritual demanded that she sit on the bell and sing sweetly to the assembled pilgrims.

One wonders, travelling back through the centuries, what gave rise to this strange and wonderful legend. What did those first people really see emerge from the mysterious waters of Rostherne Mere?

What Price a Ghost?

John Wall was born at the moated manor house of Chingle Hall, in the village of Goosnargh, near Preston, in 1620. Fifty-nine years later he was executed – hanged and quartered.

John Wall's crime was that he became a Roman Catholic priest. He was ordained in Rome, and on his return to England worked for many years in Warwickshire.

He was eventually arrested and imprisoned at Worcester Castle. At Worcester on 17 August 1679, he was condemned to death, simply for the fact of his priesthood. He was executed five days later.

In 1970, nearly three hundred years after his execution, Father John Wall became St John Wall, when canonised by the Pope as one of the Forty Martyrs of England and Wales. But, long before that, Father Wall's spirit had returned to haunt Chingle Hall, the ancient house of his birth.

All this came to light when, in June 1994, the saintly ghost of Father John and other ghosts that had since joined him in haunting his birthplace, were silent witnesses to an unusual case brought at the High Court in Liverpool.

Chingle Hall, built in 1260, was now a Grade II listed manor house, still privately owned. Since being opened to the public it had been advertised as 'reputedly the most haunted house in Britain'. It had recently changed hands, and the crux of the case before Liverpool High Court was: how much was the old, old house of ghosts worth?

The court was told that a Canadian professor and his wife had fallen in love with Chingle Hall while on holiday in 1988. They had paid £420,000 for it, hoping to further develop it as a tourist attraction. But, it was claimed, after taking possession they found that the previous owner had fed them 'pipedreams' about the profits they might make, when actually the venture was running at a loss. They admitted they had been 'gullible and naive' to enter into the sale and claimed misrepresentation by the owner and his solicitors. The owner counter-claimed, alleging breach of a business agreement.

Professor Trevor Kirkham, from Montreal, told the court he had bought the old house because he and his wife, Judy, had wanted 'something out of the ordinary'. The owner had told them that, in five years, Chingle Hall would be worth £5 million a year as a tourist attraction.

The court found in favour of the professor, awarding him £71,000 damages and compensation.

Away from the courts, as far as the ordinary visitor is concerned, there is no doubt that Chingle Hall, with its priests' holes and wealth of history and distinctly eerie air, offers very good value for money. Besides Father Wall there are some twenty other ghosts believed to be in residence, from children to a skull-faced phantom.

A case in the law courts in London in 1989 involved a whole army of ghosts. Nearly three hundred and fifty years after the Battle of Naseby, one of the most decisive battles of the English Civil War, in 1645, it was fought over again in court. And the case lost.

Villagers who had tried hard to protect the battlefield where the Parliamentary forces defeated King Charles I, were themselves defeated by Government forces when the

Court of Appeal gave the Transport Secretary the go-ahead to build a dual carriageway across the Northamptonshire battlefield. For many this was a brutal demolition of English history and desecration of the ground where thousands of men, Royalists and Roundheads, had died; and whose ghosts had been known to haunt the site.

It was at Naseby on 14 June 1645, that thirteen thousand of Oliver Cromwell's Parliamentarians opposed nine thousand Royalists led by the King. The battle, which started at 10 a.m., lasted three hours, resulting in five thousand five hundred deaths and thousands of casualties.

The King escaped, but left his State papers. Their discovery allowed the Roundheads to declare publicly that the monarchy was no longer to be trusted, because it had been in negotiation with foreign armies.

The twentieth century's local protestors fought a long battle to stop the proposed route of the M1-A1 link road, which would cut the field in two. They wanted the road to run south, avoiding the historical site. An earlier Minister of Transport, in the 1970s, agreed with them, choosing the southern route because he considered the area's historical significance to be 'of overriding importance'. But in 1987 a new Transport Minister chose the northern route instead, cutting across the middle of the battlefield. And the Appeal Court decided that it was his right to choose the route, not the court's.

That was that. No longer would people be able to meander across the battlefield exactly as it was, and no longer would the spirits of those who died there be allowed to rest in peace. The decision caused anger in the House of Lords and produced a warning from Baroness Strange, who pointed out that the battlefield was known to be haunted and this could cause considerable difficulties, with danger to traffic, if the road was built across it. But Lord Brabazon of Tara replied for the Ministry that it all depended on whether one believed in ghosts.

In the end it was a sharp attention to road building costs that ended an emotive chapter in English history – with the wry observation from the Opposition that Cromwell might have been a destructive fellow himself but even he would never have approved of such vandalism.

Six years after the Naseby decision, as a direct result of the courtroom battle, the killing fields of old England were at last afforded official protection by the Government, with the publication of a register of the forty-three most significant battlesites. Naseby was included, but too late. Too late, too, for the battlefield at Newbury, in Berkshire, the site of two bitter encounters between the forces of Cromwell and the King. And here the ghosts were quickly roused.

In December 1996, the controversial Newbury bypass was already the scene of violent skirmishes between protestors and hundreds of security men brought in by the contractors, when other forces took a hand. At least six terrified security men guarding the bypass reported seeing shadowy figures floating along the carriageway at night. The phantoms were spotted at Rickety Bridge, where many Roundhead and Cavalier soldiers were buried after the Second Battle of Newbury in 1644. Some guards said they chased the apparitions, only to see them vanish into thin air. All the men concerned were badly scared, for they were certain the apparitions were ghosts of soldiers whose graves were being disturbed. The security firm called in a chaplain to counsel the men. He said those who had seen the ghosts were level-headed young people and the Church took such things seriously.

So did a judge in the London High Court in 1988, when he was called upon to consider the case of what became known as the 'House of Horrors'. This was a council house in Nottingham where, he was told, the family had been driven from their home by a ghost which played very mournful music on an organ.

The ghost had haunted John and Helen Costello's council house for months before they left with their daughter, aged thirteen, for the safety of a guesthouse. The couple told how their daughter was brought to her knees by the sound of loud heartbeats; power plugs were pulled out, and the electric organ and a guitar were both played by themselves. Bedding was removed, a window was broken, and when a priest tried to sprinkle holy water on the stairs it was blown back over his head.

After hearing all this, Judge Michael Nolan gave the Costellos leave to appeal against a city council decision not to rehouse them. The council had claimed the couple became homeless deliberately. But the couple were backed by a spiritualist who had visited the house and found there were in fact five ghosts there, one of them 'mischievous'. Further backing came from the couple who had moved in with their three children after the Costellos moved out. The husband said lights flashed, locked doors opened and white circles with a cross inside appeared on the walls. Social workers also witnessed eerie happenings, while a retired lawyer told how he was lifted from a sofa by an unseen force.

An extraordinary case to reach the criminal courts in 1994 concerned the wrongful use of a Ouija board by jurors in a murder trial.

A man found guilty of murdering a Sussex car dealer and his wife was jailed for life at Hove Crown Court. But the *News of the World* later revealed that on the night before the verdict, which the jury spent together in a hotel, four jurors, after a drinking session, held a seance to contact the victims and so establish the identity of the killer. They made up a Ouija board using pieces of paper with letters on them. According to a troubled juror who was not at the seance, they rested their hands on an upturned glass and asked the spirits to tell them who killed the couple. The glass, answering many questions, moved across the board to spell out the accused man's name and the word 'guilty'.

Upon these revelations the Court of Appeal quashed the conviction and ordered a retrial. This was held at the Old Bailey, where the outcome was the same. The accused man was again found guilty of what the judge described as 'terrible, horrible and cold-blooded' murders for gain, and was jailed for life a second time.

Away from this forceful view taken by the courts of misuse of the Ouija board, the use of it at all continues to bring firm warnings from many quarters. They emphasise that what often starts as an experiment by the curious, a playful game, can go on to have serious consequences. It is suggested that at the very least, a Ouija board (the name is culled from the French *oui* and the German *ja*) should not be used indiscriminately and without proper supervision; and that for most people it is far better left alone, as it can become addictive. The recent findings of one Church group produced this warning: 'We find that many people using a Ouija board have become demonised, cannot sleep and keep seeing faces. They say their luck has gone badly and they are haunted.'

The Ouija board, or upturned glass, even when used responsibly, will always remain a contentious aid to investigations into the ghost world.

The Hero of Jutland

The Rev. Edward Bredin was a hero of the First World War. At the age of thirty-three he was a naval chaplain in the cruiser HMS *Warrior*, which was sunk by the Germans in the Battle of Jutland in 1916. He survived with the loss of an arm.

The reverend gentleman, who came from a good family, rose above his handicap to enjoy a long and fruitful life, living on into his nineties. In later years he became vicar of the Sussex village of Brede, and retired there.

The old clergyman was a familiar figure to the locals, one-armed, always dressed in black and often wearing a cape. He lived in Pottery Lane and was known to take a walk along that lane several times a day. One day, whilst on his perambulations, he fell in the lane and broke his hip. He died three or four days later at the age of ninety-five.

That was in 1977. Two years later Mrs Georgina Bryant, a long-time Brede resident, was walking along Pottery Lane at night with her husband, his friend, and her brother-in-law. It was ten o'clock, dark and raining, when in the headlights of a car she saw a man's figure hurry across the lane in front of her – one-armed, all in black and wearing a black cape. She saw his face, she could not mistake him. It was the late vicar. He hustled across in the direction of another cottage he owned and disappeared.

'Oh dear,' Georgina exclaimed, 'it's the Rev. Bredin!'

The others had not seen the figure, she had been walking a little in front of them. It couldn't be the old vicar, they said, he had been dead this couple of years.

But it was him, of that Georgina was very sure. Years afterwards, as she showed me the exact spot in the lane where the vicar's ghost crossed in front of her, Georgina pointed things out in simple, graphic detail. In her eighties, the startling experience of that night had never left her, it was vivid and fresh. She was frightened at the time and could not understand why the apparition had come to her, as she had had no thought of him. But she had recognised him at once; she knew the family he came from, her sister had joined them as a lady's maid and worked for them for many, many years.

On a summer's day recently Georgina and I visited Brede Church to seek out the grave of the Rev. Edward R. Bredin. We found it not in the old cemetery but in a newer burial ground parallel to it. It was a simple, neatly tended resting place for the Jutland hero. We looked at it and wondered: why did he walk that night? No one will ever know.

It was not, as it happens, Georgina Bryant's only brush with a ghost. While she was helping out with the work at a big old house at Staplecross, a few miles away, Georgina and her husband lived in a cottage in the grounds. There was a small natural lake at the rear of the cottage and she went daily past this stretch of water on her way to the big house. One night as she left her cottage to cross to the house to help in the kitchen she was petrified to see the figure of a woman in a flowing dress appear in front of her, then float over the lake and away. On reaching the house in some distress, Georgina blurted out to a daughter of the family what she had seen, 'plain as plain', but the lady was not a bit surprised. 'Oh, yes,' she said, 'several people have seen her. We call her the "Lady of the Lake"!'

More was to come. She told Georgina quite matter-of-factly that one of the bedrooms in the house was haunted by a tall, stately man. One of the other daughters had slept there and awoken to see the man standing over her. Another daughter had laughed at the very idea of a ghost and said she wasn't afraid to sleep there, but after a couple of nights she, too, awoke with a start and screamed as a man just as described leaned over and made to touch her. She ran from the room and no one had used it since.

Ghosts seemed to follow Georgina around. Even on holiday. On going to stay with a friend in Essex she came down after a good night's sleep and said to her friend, 'Oh, what a lovely smell. I can smell pipe smoke, someone's smoking a pipe.' But her friend shook her head. 'No,' she said, 'we don't smoke at all.' Georgina was puzzled. 'But I can smell it, it's all around me,' she protested. Her friend laughed. 'No, we've had this happen before,' she said.

She then told Georgina the story of the smoky haunting. The house had been built on the site of what had been a tobacconist's shop. The old man who owned the shop, worked there for many years and died there, had always smoked a pipe and it seemed he could not bear to leave the old place, for although they themselves were not affected, a number of visitors to the house had smelt the smoking ghost.

Then there is the matter of the Giant of Brede, although here we touch upon an age-old legend and a rather bloodthirsty one. The story is that in ancient times a giant used to come from Brede Church along a tunnel under an old bridge, and kill a baby in the village. If you stood on the bridge at midnight you could hear ghostly groans and see a ghost appear.

Well, Georgina's late husband, Ernest, a lorry driver, used the route across the 'Groaning Bridge' as a short cut to his grandmother's cottage at Broadlands, where he stayed, and he heard the ghostly noises several times as he crossed it. And when Georgina gives you that direct, no-nonsense look, you know he most assuredly did.

The old bridge was constructed over a deep cutting. It

is built over now to afford a higher, modern roadway, but underneath it all parts of the original bridge remain, including the tunnel through which the Giant of Brede was said to go to and fro on his dreadful errand.

If you travel over the bridge and up the hill you come to Brede Place, and here you leave legend for fact, as all the village knows. Brede Place was home to the Frewen family, cousins of Sir Winston Churchill. During the Second World War, Georgina told me, Commander Frewen brought a servant home with him, a black man, and they put him in a room purported to be haunted. The poor man stayed there one night, left screaming and would not go into it again. A woman had committed suicide there many years before and the servant swore he had seen the ghost of the dead woman.

On a sombre personal note, Georgina told me of the recent frightening experience of a friend's son as he was driving under the Harrow Arch, situated on the northern rim of Hastings. He was driving alone in his car on a dark evening when, as he drove under the bridge, something, 'a person', suddenly came in front of the car. It was so vivid he stopped the car quickly and got out, trembling, thinking he had knocked somebody down and fully expecting to find a body lying there. But there was no one.

The bridge has a bad reputation, Georgina said. A number of years ago the son of another friend of hers committed suicide there by throwing himself off the bridge. Others had died there in the same way, crashing to the road below. It could be that their unfortunate spirits still walked.

Originally a northern girl, hailing from Shotley Bridge, Georgina also told me of the strange incident at a haunted house in Northumberland, the actual event being even weirder than the haunting itself. Her elder sister, who was a young girl at the time, well remembers the happening at Hatton Hall, Otterburn, before the First World War.

On a dark, wet night, while the owner was away and

only the butler and housekeeper in residence, there came a loud rapping of the heavy knocker on the front door of Hatton Hall. The butler opened the door to find two men standing there with a huge trunk. They said they had come from the Tyne and had been told to deliver the trunk to Hatton Hall. 'You had better bring it in,' the butler told them. The men carried it with difficulty into the hall and left, and the butler locked up and went to bed. Next morning, he got up to find blood running down the hall ... They never did discover the identity of the body in the trunk.

Canon to the Rescue

The stocky, middle-aged gentleman in a crumpled green tweed suit and black duffle coat did not look like a 'ghostbuster', much less like a pillar of the Church of England, but in fact he was both. The clue lay in the 'luggage' he carried – a tape recorder, canonical robes and portable Communion set. Canon John Pearce-Higgins, Vice-Provost of Southwark Cathedral, was off to keep another date with a ghost.

He made hundreds of such visits during the 1960s and 1970s, and not only in his own Southwark diocese and other parts of London. One day he might be at a haunted house in Hackney; another would find him at a village pub in Suffolk, holding a Communion service to rid it of an unwanted ghost.

Canon Pearce-Higgins, vice-chairman of the Churches' Fellowship for Psychical and Spiritual Studies, did not profess to having any special psychical abilities himself, but worked in partnership with a medium. The medium would seek to determine the cause of the haunting and endeavour to contact the recalcitrant spirit; the Canon handled the religious side of things, supplying the service or Requiem Mass to give the spirit earthly release.

I had occasion to speak to Canon Pearce-Higgins just after he had been to a terraced house in Chatham and successfully disposed of an old yellow-faced ghost in boots who had stamped about the house, persecuting the family and tickling the wife's feet in bed.

The Fellowship had run into a great deal of opposition from the bishops when it was formed, but times were changing. The Bishop of London was among its patrons and its vice-president was the Bishop of Southwark, Dr Mervyn Stockwood. Dr Stockwood's view had been openly stated: 'I have no patience with people who write the whole thing off as humbug and fraud. The work the Fellowship is doing is important because it is a subject which demands careful and thoughtful inquiry. The weakness of the Church has been its refusal to consider the evidence or discuss it.'

Canon Pearce-Higgins, formerly vicar of Putney, was one of the few churchmen who was a convinced spiritualist. He accepted almost all the spiritualist philosophy of death. He said it explained the New Testament, the Resurrection, the 'many mansions' of God's house and the miracles, and it was his wish to see the established churches acknowledging it.

An ex-Army chaplain, an extremely practical man, he explained to me that the ghosts he dealt with came from all walks of life. They could be those of people who had died suddenly or violently, or were too attached to the things they had left behind. They usually made their presence felt when someone sensitive or psychic invaded their haunted space.

'If you die in bed,' he said, 'you know what has happened, and you pass on. If you are suddenly cut off in the prime of life you can find yourself wandering about without anyone taking any notice of you.'

The ghosts' actions tended to reflect their characters when alive. Hence some were quite harmless, some a nuisance, and others spiteful or violent. Whatever their behaviour they had got stuck here, bewildered and perplexed.

'I blame the churches,' the Canon said forcibly, 'they

don't tell people what happens when they die. They teach that they are buried and wait for resurrection, bones, worms and all.'

He explained that everyone, according to the spiritualists, had a spirit guide. They looked after you, worried about you, wanted to see you behaving yourself, but were generally incommunicado. But if you were a medium, then you could talk to them. It was they who performed the healing, the assistance to the 'lost' souls of ghosts. If you died violently, the spirits came and tried to help you over. Otherwise, people killed in air crashes would be wandering around hopelessly for an eternity. When a person resisted the guides, they stayed loitering, kicking over the traces of their life, trying to talk to the people they knew but failing to make anyone see or recognise them.

All the ghosts he had dealt with were not sudden, sporadic affairs. For instance, one south London couple who sought his help had suffered the attentions of a ghost for so long that they had even considered putting him down on their census form. Officially, anyone living in the house had to be entered on the form – and 'Joe' had been resident with them for no less than eighteen years.

The couple, Maisie and Fred Batchelor, told the Canon how Joe, flitting around like a shadow, had messed up their lives in their three-bedroomed home at New Cross. He pulled furniture around, opened doors, dragged his feet in the front bedroom, and called out in the middle of the night from the foot of their bed. Several times he had actually shown up in the bedroom wearing a white see-through shroud and a black headdress – 'just like a nun', Maisie described it.

The Canon and his partner, the medium Donald Page, finally got Joe to go, though not without a struggle. A flower pot aimed by an unseen hand crashed to the floor inches from Maisie just before the ceremony began. Then, much to her relief, it was all over. The neighbours had thought her mad but now she had been proved right. Joe's identity, however, remained a mystery. All the medium could discover was that he had a big wound on the side of his head. It could have been caused by him falling downstairs.

One of Canon Pearce-Higgins's most memorable out-of-town cases was that of a house in Nottingham, once a vicarage, that was reputed to be haunted by a monk. A widow bought the house and almost immediately was troubled by heavy thumps and banging noises, doors that creaked open and closed. The widow's schoolboy sons referred to the unruly spirit as 'Ebenezer' and tried to get used to him, but the noises became more gruesome: the piano began to play with no one seated at the keyboard, books in the children's room were flung about for no apparent reason and finally the widow received a severe shock one night when an ectoplasmic cloud moved across the room accompanied by eerie wails and ghastly shrieking.

With the aid of his medium partner, the Canon discovered that there had been a tragedy in the house, which had been used as a refectory by monks in the reign of King Henry VIII.

'A servant girl was made pregnant by a monk from a monastery nearby and had been imprisoned in the attic of the house. Her baby was taken away and murdered, and later she was poisoned. We discovered the name of the girl and I spoke to her through the medium. We discovered two monks, one the father of the girl's baby daughter and the other the one who murdered the baby, and I spoke to both of them.'

After the Canon's service of blessing, prayers and celebration of Holy Communion both monks were eventually persuaded to leave, but still certain phenomena remained. 'There was a smell of tobacco smoke, and the mystery of the piano that played by itself. The tobacco smell we discovered was caused by an old tramp and his friends who had used the place when it was derelict. They had been dead for some time, but we made contact and persuaded them to leave also.

'It was the widow herself who helped to solve the piano mystery. One day she saw the apparition of a woman dressed in Edwardian clothes at the piano. She had an idea and checked through old photographs with the village schoolmistress and they discovered the identity of the Edwardian figure. It was the second wife of a vicar who had been an incumbent years before.'

After this last of the spirits was prevailed upon to leave, the house enjoyed its first peace for five years.

The Canon said he would sometimes come upon people who had tried to communicate with spirits by means of the Ouija board. He was strongly against this. No one should try to develop psychic powers on their own account – not without strict supervision. Once anyone tried to open their subconscious mind by such things as automatic writing, the Ouija board and table-turning with glass and alphabet, they had no idea what forces they may be admitting.

Away from the ghosts of everyday hauntings, Canon Pearce-Higgins had this fascinating story to tell of the Rev. Maurice Elliott, Vicar of Itchenor in Sussex, who was one of the pioneer figures in the Fellowship for Psychical and Spiritual Studies.

Mr Elliott and his wife had longed for a child. Yet not only could she not have one, but she was also due for a serious operation which might endanger her life.

One evening in despair, as they knelt to pray, an angel appeared. They described his presence as 'dazzling white'. They both saw him at once. The angel gave them a message of exact information. They had to pack up and go to a certain hotel in Bournemouth near the beach, which was described exactly. There they would meet someone, again minutely described, who would help them.

They set off and soon found the hotel, 'guided to it by

the angel', to use their own words, and at dinner that night they sat next to a man who exactly tallied with the description given by the angel. They exchanged glances but did not dare to speak to him at first. Only when Maurice Elliott discovered he was a well-known West End surgeon was he certain he had the right man. In the lounge after dinner, Elliott diffidently approached him and told him the story of his wife. He carefully omitted the vision of the angel because he thought a sceptical medical man might laugh. The surgeon listened to the story and said, 'Look, I'll see your wife and examine her.' When he did so, he contradicted all the other gloomy medical reports and said: 'Not only does your wife not need an operation, but she can have a baby. I believe she will have one within twelve months.'

At this, the clergyman blurted out his story of the angel. Instead of sneering, the surgeon said gently, 'That accounts for it. Do you know, I had an overwhelming compulsion to go to the hotel at that particular time? I can't explain it. But I felt as if I were being directed there because I had a strange feeling someone needed my help.'

Canon Pearce-Higgins, in concluding this story, told me, 'Of course, there are sceptics of the Elliotts' experience. Yet that baby, a baby girl, was born just as had been predicted. She was baptised at Winchester Cathedral and appropriately named Dorothea – which means "the gift of God". And she is now a grown-up, happily married woman with four sons.'

The Trouble with Amy

A titled lady was found lying dead at the foot of the stairs with her neck broken. Did she fall? Or was she pushed?

Four hundred years after the tragedy the question is still asked. The unfortunate lady was Lady Dudley, better known and remembered by her maiden name of Amy Robsart.

Amy's story, and that of her remarkably persistent ghost, has a royal beginning, evolving from court intrigues following the death of Henry VIII.

Henry had two children by his first wife, Catherine of Aragon, a boy and a girl: Edward and Mary. On Henry's death in 1547 the boy, his only son, ascended the throne as Edward VI. He was nine years old.

The strong man behind the throne at this time was John Dudley, Duke of Northumberland. One of his sons, Robert Dudley, courted young and attractive Amy Robsart. She was a Norfolk girl, the daughter of Sir John Robsart. He was Lord of the Manor of Syderstone, a village twelve miles inland from Hunstanton. The family lived some miles away at Stanfield Hall, where Amy grew up.

Robert Dudley and Amy Robsart were married at Sheen, Surrey, in 1550. Edward VI, in the third year of his reign and still only eleven years old, kept a little diary in which he made this quaint note of the event:

'1550. June 4. Sir Robert Dudeley, third sonne to th' Erle of Warwick, married S. Jon. Robsarte's daughter, after wich mariage, ther were certain gentlemen that did strive who shuld first take away a goose's head which was hanged alive on two cross posts.'

Shortly after her marriage Amy, now Lady Dudley, made her home at Syderstone Hall. The local rectory was situated close by. She and her husband appear to have lived happily together at first, but events moved rapidly at court. The boy King suffered from galloping consumption and after only seven years' reign was near death. The rightful successor to the throne was his sister, Mary, but the Duke of Northumberland, as Regent, persuaded the dying Edward to exclude Mary on the grounds of her religion: she was a staunch Catholic. The Duke succeeded in naming the Protestant Lady Jane Grey in her stead. Lady Jane was the grand-daughter of a sister of Henry VIII; she also just happened to be the Duke's daughter-in-law, being married to another of his sons, Guildford Dudley.

But Amy saw her scheming father-in-law's coup collapse.

Edward VI died in 1553, aged sixteen. Lady Jane Grey, also only sixteen, ascended the throne. But she reigned for only nine days. Mary entered London with her supporters; the people were anxious to keep a Tudor on the throne. The Duke of Northumberland was seized and executed, poor Lady Jane and her husband meeting a similar fate the following year.

Only three years wed and Amy Robsart had lost her father-in-law and a brother-in-law to the block. Her husband was seized and imprisoned too, but released a year later. Robert Dudley proved to be much better at survival than his late father. He rode out the rest of Mary's short, bloody reign, till her early death in 1558, and came splendidly into his own when she was followed on the throne by Elizabeth, daughter of Henry VIII and Ann

Boleyn. Robert Dudley swiftly became a handsome favourite of the young Elizabeth I; they were both in their twenties. Too much of a favourite, claimed his critics among the ordinary folk, who accused him of neglecting his wife to make overtures to the Queen. Early in 1560 Amy moved from Syderstone to stay at Cumnor Hall, Berkshire, the home of a friend of her husband's. Gossip said that Robert deliberately left her behind at Cumnor because she stood in the way of his ambitions. And it was here at Cumnor that same year that Amy met her death.

The facts emerged from evidence given at the inquest.

It was Sunday, 8 September 1560. Lady Dudley told all her household to go and enjoy themselves at Abingdon Fair. A Mrs Odingsell, her companion, remonstrated with her, saying that the day was not a proper one for decent folk to go to a fair, but her ladyship grew very angry at this, insisting that all her people should go. And so they went, leaving only Lady Dudley and two other women in the house. On the servants' return, the luckless lady was found lying dead at the bottom of a flight of stairs.

Although the inquest jury returned a verdict of accidental death, there remained an air of mystery about it all. Did Amy really fall? Or was it suicide? Or was she murdered? A cloud of suspicion hung over the whole affair. Despite the legal verdict, Robert Dudley was believed by many to be responsible for his wife's death, perhaps even hiring assassins to engineer it, so that he might make his proposal to the Queen. (This latter belief receives some support from documents discovered later, which indicate that a plot to poison her was actually entered into before her death.)

The depth of feeling about Amy Robsart's death was widespread. There must have been something charismatic about Amy, besides something wanting about her husband, to account for the steadfast belief that she had been wrongly done by.

However, Robert Dudley, though stalked by the

shadows of suspicion, continued to do well at court, despite his imaginings of becoming the Queen's consort being dashed. He was made Knight of the Garter, Baron Dudley; and, three years after his wife's death, the Queen made him Earl of Leicester. He prospered on into his fifties, advocating strong measures against Catholics and Spain. Even so, as late as 1584, four years before his death, a book was published containing accusations against him regarding Amy's death. It was publicly condemned by the Privy Council as an infamous and scandalous libel, and Leicester went off on an expedition to the Netherlands.

Now for the first appearance of Amy's ghost.

In 1588, while staying at Cornbury Park, in Oxfordshire, Robert Dudley went hunting in Wychwood Forest and, it was recorded, came face to face with the spirit of his dead wife. She warned him that he would be with her in ten days. He returned to the house, fell ill and died within the time stated.

Once at large, Amy's ghost continued to roam Cornbury Park. But she also haunted Cumnor Hall, miles to the south. In particular there were frequent sightings of her on the staircase down which she had fallen to her death. Her appearances at Cumnor, both in the hall and in the park, went on for many years, until finally a number of clergymen joined forces in an attempt to lay the restless ghost. Some accounts say that nine, others that twelve clergymen from Oxford and surrounds were involved in the ceremony, which took place at a pond, known ever afterwards as 'Madam Dudley's Pond'. It was commonly said that the water in the pond was never known to freeze over again. However, Amy Robsart's apparition did not cease to walk. It still appeared at intervals, even after Cumnor Hall was pulled down in 1810.

The story of Amy's alleged murder and her wandering ghost had attracted writers like Mickle, who popularised her in his ballad *Cumnor Hall*:

'And in that Manor now no more
　　Is cheerful feast and sprightly ball;
For ever, since that dreary hour,
　　Have spirits haunted Cumnor Hall.

'The village maids, with fearful glance,
　　Avoid the ancient mossgrown wall;
Nor ever lead the merry dance,
　　Among the groves of Cumnor Hall.

'Full many a traveller oft hath sighed
　　And pensive wept the countess's fall,
As, wandering onward, they espied
　　The haunted towers of Cumnor Hall.'

Shortly after Cumnor Hall was demolished, Sir Walter Scott seized upon Amy's suspected foul murder of two hunded and fifty years ago to create an extravagant piece of fiction. In *Kenilworth*, published in 1821, he gave a highly dramatic but purely imaginative account of her tragic death. This was no simple push down the stairs, but a most ingenious act of homicide.

Amy was described in *Kenilworth* as being imprisoned in an isolated tower, approached only by a narrow drawbridge. Halfway across this drawbridge was a trap door, so arranged that anyone stepping on it would be pitched below into a darksome abyss. Varney, the chief villain of the novel, rode into the courtyard and gave a peculiar kind of whistle, which Amy recognised and, thinking her husband was coming, rushed out, stepped on the trap door and fell headlong down.

'Look down into the vault,' says Varney to Foster, his companion, 'what seest thou?' 'I see only a heap of white clothes, like a snowdrift,' said Foster. 'Oh, God! she moves her arm!' 'Hurl something down upon her: thy gold-chest, Tony, it is a heavy one ...'

Only a few years after the publication of *Kenilworth*,

with its lurid flights of fancy, the Amy Robsart story was plunged back into reality with one of the more astonishing outbreaks of ghostly activity recorded in the nineteenth century.

It seems that Amy Robsart's ghost had chosen a new haunt, taking up residence in the rectory at Syderstone which her old home, Syderstone Hall, had adjoined. She was occasionally seen prowling about the dark corridors and rooms of the old rectory, a shadowy figure in white. Windows locked and bolted at night were often found flapping open in the morning. People passing the rectory after dark said they had seen Amy leaning out of a window, gazing into the moonlight, as if expecting to see someone who had promised to visit her. At other times she was seen wandering about the grounds. One villager who encountered her said she was wearing a short white jacket and silk petticoat and went flitting by her with a sort of gasping sob.

In time, Amy's ghost had come to be looked upon by most folk as just a part of village life; a harmless, even friendly, spirit. But, suddenly and unaccountably, her chosen haunt seemed to be invaded by another, more unruly spirit – or perhaps even several of them – as the rectory became a hotbed of supernatural activity.

In 1833, with reports of the bizarre events published in local newspapers, everything that had been bottled up before came tumbling out. The evidence was voluminous and overwhelming. There were statements by various clergymen and eminent gentlemen; exchanges of corroborative letters; and declaration after declaration made before magistrates by those who had heard and witnessed the mysterious happenings at the rectory. They included villagers, tradespeople and servants, some of whom, unable to write their name, legally signed the statements with their mark (X).

The peak of activity was reached soon after the Rev. John Stewart and his family took up residence at

Syderstone Rectory (it had been unoccupied for two years previously). Articles were thrown about and bells rung; doors and windows opened and shut themselves; furniture was shifted around; there was the sound as of a huge wrecker's ball descending upon the roof and penetrating to the ground floor; another sound like a shower of copper coins falling; screams, as of a human being under torture; the rattling of iron and clashing of glass; incessant loud and violent knocking; and shrieks, not coming from any wall but hovering frighteningly in the atmosphere of the room and being heard by everyone.

There was nightly uproar. The terror of the servants became intense. A gardener and a maid both refused to sleep in the house any longer; another servant simply upped and left; while Miss Stewart, the Rector's daughter, after shifting her quarters from one bedroom to another, finally took refuge in the house of a neighbour.

On one occasion Miss Stewart saw the ghost of Amy. It came to her, bending over her bed, peering at her, so close that the side of the bed hid the lower part of its body. It stood in front of her for a few moments and then floated backwards. Miss Stewart was alarmed to see that the body was unfinished, not quite having human substance. But, she said, the face was perfect, a beautiful but tragic-looking face. The face of a very unhappy woman.

Miss Stewart dragged herself upright in bed suddenly and challenged the apparition: 'Madam! What are you doing in my room?' At her cry, Amy disappeared, sucked back into the mistiness from which she had emerged. Moments later ghostly laughter was heard in all parts of the house.

Two friends of her father who later kept watch in the girl's room heard clawing behind the oak panelling, as of a big cat; low moaning of someone in anguish; and repeated knocks in the wall, the noise of which shook the bed. But there was much, much more.

The Rector and his family, including his two eldest

boys, together with four clergymen from other parishes and a doctor and his wife, sat up one night and were treated with ghostly noises that lasted with little peace till two hours after dawn. The sitters each wrote fully of their experience. And as one recorded on the lighter side: 'On one occasion the ghost was asked to give ten knocks. It gave nine and, as if recollecting itself that the number was not completed, it began again and gave ten. I also heard it beat time to the air of the verse of a song sung by Miss Stewart – if I mistake not, "Home, Sweet Home".'

The ghost seemed to be attracted to the daughter. Sometimes, on preparing for bed, Miss Stewart would sing the evening hymn, at which taps would be heard on the woodwork of the bed, beating time to the music. The perpetual disturbances made the Rector's wife ill. Magistrates, clergy and surrounding gentry called daily at the rectory to offer their services. Finally, sympathy – and some scepticism – was substituted by action. The Marquis of Cholmondley, patron of the living, ordered the ground round the house to be excavated. A trench was dug round the back of the house and borings made in other parts to a depth of six or seven feet, but nothing was found, no vault or underground communication with the walls which might have been responsible for at least some of the rackety noises.

Now stern action was taken. Two Bow Street officers specially brought up from London kept a watchful night armed with loaded pistols in rooms opposite to one another. Upon each hearing noises they rushed out with pistols at the ready – and narrowly missed shooting each other.

All the disturbances had come to a head when Mr Stewart had only been in the house a little over twelve months, but it was now established that noises of sorts, and some manifestations, had in fact been heard and seen in the house at intervals for at least the past thirty years, if not longer. Some local people were convinced that the spirit of

THE TROUBLE WITH AMY

a rector of some forty years ago had a part in the hauntings; others thought there could well be unknown, alien forces at work besides this ghost and that of Amy Robsart, who was not held responsible for the direst unearthly sounds. But whatever the causes of the various disturbances, they eventually seemed to lessen and ultimately disperse altogether when the old rectory was pulled down in 1850.

Whether Amy Robsart's ghost continued to walk at Syderstone after that is not clear, though it was seen at Cumnor, after Cumnor Hall's demolition in 1810. Meanwhile there was her third haunt, that of Cornbury Park. There she did continue to roam, and the tradition grew that her appearance was a warning of sudden death, as it had been to her husband, and that whoever met her at nightfall knew that their time had come, whatever their state of health. Sightings of Amy at Cornbury were reported at intervals up to the start of the Second World War.

Whether or not the ubiquitous ghost of Amy Robsart still lingers on, one thing is certain: her extraordinary story will never be forgotten.

Spirits at the Inn

There are hundreds of haunted hotels, inns and public houses in Britain. There is no precise figure, as some hauntings come and go, while others, being a nuisance, are got rid of; but, generally speaking, a haunting is seldom bad for trade. Some hotel groups have a special leaflet listing haunted premises. There are also local pub guides and the like. But most information about our haunted inns seems to go abroad, for the benefit of foreign visitors. The British Tourist Authority, for instance, supplies its agencies in the USA with an informal list of hotels with a haunting history, unfortunately not obtainable in this country.

Ghostly guests at the inn take on a variety of guises. Many are unknowns, such as a lady in white wandering the bedrooms, monks carousing in the cellars, or something supernatural haunting the corridors.

There are gentle ghosts, like 'Lady Jane', who haunts the Dalston Hall Hotel in Carlisle. She is the spirit of a sixteenth-century serving wench described as 'dead houseproud', since she hates having her home changed around. She is more often sensed and felt, rather than seen.

Some licensed premises have desperate characters in attendance. The sixteenth-century Finnygook Inn, at Crafthole, Cornwall, is reputed to be haunted by Finny the Smuggler, one of a band of smugglers who were active on that part of the Cornish coast; while Edward Higgins, a highwayman who went to the gallows in 1767, is said to haunt the Royal George Hotel in his home town of Knutsford, Cheshire.

Some hostelries have more than one ghost, like the Scole Inn, near Diss, Norfolk. Here, at this coaching inn dating from 1665, the main ghost is that of a woman murdered by her jealous husband, who falsely accused her of adultery. She is said to be quite harmless, as are the other two ghosts listed in the hotel's brochure: a little boy down in the cellar, and a restless spirit in the kitchen. These resident ghosts have been seen a dozen times in recent years.

On the grisly side, a singularly eerie haunting is attributed to the seventeenth-century Ship Inn at Brandon Creek, near Southery, Norfolk. Here, it is recorded, were based three Irish prisoners captured during the English Civil War who were among others employed as 'slave labour' on fen drainage schemes. One night the trio murdered the Dutch couple who ran the inn and made their escape into the Fens. When ultimately tracked down and caught, they were sentenced to be hanged in peculiarly Fenland fashion: the noose was attached to a gibbet in the river with the free end tied to a barge. As the tide went out, so the barge dropped lower in the water until the men slowly strangled. There have been reports of shocked travellers seeing dim, wriggling shapes in mid-air just beyond the Ship Inn's riverside gardens.

Landlords and owners change, but many ghosts go on for ever, particularly those of the historical kind. A case in point is the Talbot Hotel at Oundle, Northamptonshire, where Mary Queen of Scots is said to have been seen or sensed on the staircase. Not that she ever slept or drank at the Talbot; the inn did not exist in the lifetime of that unfortunate queen. It was built forty years after her death. How it came to acquire Mary's ghost is a story in itself.

Mary Queen of Scots was last imprisoned in

Fotheringhay Castle, just a few miles down the road from Oundle. There she was executed for treason in 1587.

Poor Mary's belongings went far and wide: a gilt and silver box in which she kept letters, her prayer book and gold rosary, the last chair she sat on, even the chemise she wore on the scaffold, and, of course, her death mask. But something rather more solid found its way to the Talbot Hotel when it was built, and this was the staircase from Fotheringhay Castle. The castle itself was demolished and only the mound remains, but it seems that Mary's ghost came to the Talbot along with the staircase. It is said that the outline of a crown in the wood of the balustrade was made by her ring as she gripped the rail on her way to the execution block.

A dormant ghost at the four hundred-year-old Globe Hotel, Ludlow, Shropshire, roused itself in the 1950s, much to the alarm of two young wives. An RAF airman and his wife who moved into a flat on the premises began to hear unusual noises coming from a disused room above them. They made enquiries but were unable to find an explanation for the noises, which they found very disturbing. Then another airman and his wife moved into an adjoining flat. One evening, while their husbands were on duty at the nearby RAF camp, the two wives were sitting in the living room of one of the flats when they were shocked to see standing by the doorway the figure of a man clad in a cloak and wig. He disappeared.

After that there were more unexplained noises and instances of articles being mysteriously moved around in the flats. When the couples made more enquiries they discovered that earlier tenants of the flats had experienced similar happenings.

The ghost was finally identified. It was believed to be that of a former soldier at Ludlow Castle who died in a room at the hotel in the sixteenth century. He is thought to be still around, having a particularly unnerving penchant for breathing down ladies' necks.

The Shipwright's Arms, a fascinating old pub found down a mud track over bleak marshland at Faversham, Kent, is haunted by a Dutch sea captain whose ship foundered in a nearby creek. It is said the captain knocked at the door of the weather-boarded inn, but closing time had been called. The publican shouted from a bedroom window that the place was closed and, forced to stay outside all night, the poor captain died of exposure.

The remains of the master's boat lie across the creek and his ghost continues to haunt the inn that refused him succour. They know when he is about for there is a sudden overpowering smell of rum and tobacco. Sometimes, his aggrieved spirit won't let anyone open the door.

This business of ghosts wilfully interfering with doors is not uncommon, but I must mention one of the more extreme cases known to me. This happened at the Half Moon Hotel, at Clare, Suffolk, in the 1950s.

Mr and Mrs Reg Brock knew within hours of taking over the old coaching inn that something was not quite right. They became aware of the ghost on their first night at the inn, when they were woken up by the sound of a dice being thrown by an invisible player. The second night they were both aroused again when every door in the place slammed shut. This was followed by the sound of running feet. Regularly, the bed in one of the spare rooms was found with the coverlet turned down and the impression of a head and body on the sheets.

Mrs Brock told me that when she was in bed she could see the ghost's shadow going backwards and forwards under the bedroom door as it walked up and down the landing. The Half Moon, more than four hundred years old, had everything expected of such a venerable building, from a cellar once used as a church to a priest's hole, hidden cupboards and a secret room; but there was no clue as to the likely identity of the spectral visitor. The Brocks resigned themselves to months of irritating disturbances, but then the ghost went too far. One night after opening time they waited patiently for the first customer. But no one came. Later, they found the reason: the front door had been bolted, presumably by the ghost. After that they kept a pretty fierce eye on that door.

Within a few months of taking over the Royal Oak at Upton Snodsbury, near Worcester, back in the 1960s, the new landlord found he had a resident ghost haunting a room above the bar. But this was a ghost with a difference. It was that of a baby, whimpering and crying – most eerie and frightening.

The landlord, Mr P. W. James, told me that the sound, which could be heard about once a month, was just like a baby whimpering on being disturbed and then giving a surprised scream. It stopped suddenly as if cut off.

On making enquiries Mr James found that when the inn had been renovated three years earlier, extensions had included the conversion of a group of adjoining cottages. It was in one of these cottages that a father had returned home late one night in the 1750s, and in a fit of anger threw a baby girl out of the window. The baby died and the father was hanged for murder.

It was evident that the haunting had persisted for some time. Mr James said that when he mentioned the ghost to one of his staff from the village she replied that they hadn't told him of it before in case he did not like living in a haunted house.

Mr James decided he could not put up with the pitiful ghost because of its unhappy and troubled cry. He called in the local vicar to help release the baby's spirit from the premises.

About this time there was an outburst of haunting at a pub in London, which also had a feasible explanation, although one dating from more recent times.

Staff at the King's Arms in Rye Lane, Peckham, named their ghost 'Gertie'. Coincidentally, the troubles began when Mr and Mrs Anthony King took over as managers. The next three months were near chaotic, and the couple could find no reasonable explanation for the upsets. Objects of all kinds were found scattered in odd places, strange footsteps were heard in the dead of night, and staff complained of the sensation of someone tapping them on the shoulder. The chief chef refused to go down into the cellar after seeing 'something', while the Kings' dog often careered around the inn barking wildly for no reason. Then Mrs King found childlike scrawling of the word 'piano' on the baby grand in the living room, yet there were no children in the house.

The pub had been rebuilt eleven years earlier after being bombed during the Second World War, and after many enquiries the Kings were left wondering if the haunting was connected with the eleven people who died in the old King's Arms when the bomb fell on it during an air raid in 1940. I understand the haunting did finally subside, although the ghostly tapping on the shoulder persisted for some time.

Soon after actor Michael Elphick, the star of television's *Boon*, bought the lease of a picture-postcard country inn in Warwickshire, he found he had also bought what appeared to be a resident ghost. Startled customers at the White Swan, at Henley-in-Arden, told of seeing a young woman in a flowing dress moving across a landing. This happened several times.

The actor invited members of the local ghost society to keep a vigil in the fourteenth-century hotel in an attempt to solve the mystery. They did so, spending a weekend on watch, staying in the room nearest to the spot where the ghostly woman had been seen, but were unable to come up with an explanation. The ghost continued to walk the landing and unnerve guests by tugging at their bedclothes and suddenly locking the door of the haunted room.

Michael Elphick then called in a psychic investigator, Graham Wyley. He detected ghostly activity in the room and, during the night, witnessed the ghost of a sad-eyed young woman. On searching local records he found that a young serving girl named Virginia Black had died in the hotel one hundred and fifty years earlier. She broke her neck when she fell down the stairs to her attic bedroom during a row with her boyfriend, who was later hanged.

The ghost having been traced, guests were told about Virginia before they slept in the room, and this seemed to settle things, for there were no more sightings.

Down at another old pub, in Surrey, they dubbed their ghost 'Thumper', for thump he did, all the way through the White Bear at Fickleshole. He tramped through the rafters and stairways of the rambling Tudor building. Door latches clicked and stairs creaked eerily, awaking the sleeping household. Licensee Bill Dixon and his wife, Marie, who faced this new outbreak of ghostly activity in the 1970s, learned that the ghost had actually been around for many years, though no one knew why it should suddenly resume its nocturnal activities.

Mrs Dixon christened the ghost Thumper because of the noise it made when going through the building. She would be woken by what were definitely footsteps across the ceiling of her bedroom. Nor were its activities confined to the pub. Two young barmen who lived in connecting cottages, two hundred years old, were also wakened by doors mysteriously opening and closing. When they investigated they saw nothing, but heard footsteps sounding away in the direction of the inn.

The Dixons were satisfied that the noisy ghost, which tended to really disturb their sleep about every two months, was not harmful to them. Even their dogs did not seem unduly alarmed. The big puzzle was, who could Thumper possibly be?

Mr Dixon went through parish records, but nothing he saw showed any foul deeds being done, or tragedies occurring, that could have caused a tormented soul to linger beneath the roof of the White Bear. There was, however, one extra thought. The oak beams in the inn were known to have come from an old sailing ship. Could it be that some ancient mariner had followed the remains of his ship to their last resting place?

My newspaper colleague, John Dodd, came upon the story of Mrs Lizzie Lawton in the 1970s. Who was Lizzie Lawton? She was the landlady of the Angel Inn at Lyme Regis, Dorset. She loved her pub, but in the 1920s had to leave it, and when she died it was not her last home that her ghost returned to haunt, it was her beloved Angel Inn.

Lizzie proved a jealous spirit who could not stand other people running her pub. She haunted successive licensees over the years, finally making a personal appearance to one in 1968, in broad daylight.

Landlord Gordon Hosie was taking an afternoon nap on his bed. He looked up, and there, standing over his bed, was a little old lady. She was dressed like Queen Victoria, with a bun in her hair, a white apron on, and plenty of jewellery. She stood looking down at him for a few minutes, then disappeared into a wardrobe. Mr Hosie was considerably upset and, although afraid of being laughed at, confessed to neighbours living across the road from the Angel what he had seen. They recognised old Mrs Lawton at once. Mrs Elsie Clark remembered her as a lovely woman, very kind, and very old fashioned. She said Lizzie always wore Victorian clothes, with a bun at the back of her hair, and a white apron.

Lizzie never wanted to leave the pub, Mrs Clark said, but her daughter could not cope with it, so they moved. Lizzie was heard to say at the time, 'Nobody's going to do the same here as I've done.' It was a sort of curse, so unlike her, but she felt so strongly about her pub, and she certainly returned after death to make her presence felt to newcomers having the effrontery to stand behind her bar – particularly women. It was commonly said that Lizzie didn't mind men but couldn't stand women.

Mr Hosie died a few months after seeing Lizzie that fateful afternoon, but that was not the end of the haunting. Lizzie Lawton seemed intent on hanging around to startle new tenants by sending glasses flying from shelves to shatter at their feet, smashing crockery into smithereens with tremendous force, and similar inexplicable capers.

It should be said that all pub ghosts are not years old. The Lazy Toad pub-discotheque in Beckenham, Kent, has a very modern ghost. According to reports, it is that of an unhappy looking teenage girl said to walk the road outside, then vanish. She wears early 1980s clothing and is dressed as if it were summer.

Inn ghosts are not often really violent, though it was the misfortune of a Northumberland publican to be assailed by one. The malevolent spirit at the Galleon, Spittal, frightened a man in the loo and appeared at the bar. It shut off taps and switches and called out 'Christine' to landlord Keith Mooney's wife. Then it went over the top and tried to kill him with a full beer barrel. It hurled the eighty-eight-pint keg at him in the cellar, smashing a door frame. Terrified Mr Mooney, who had to call in a priest to banish the evil spirit, was reported to have lost four stone in weight with worry.

One publican did not wait for help but quit his haunted pub there and then. Landlord Hayden Rowlett walked out of the Globe, in Bedford, during the summer of 1997, claiming it to be haunted by the American band leader Glenn Miller, who died during the Second World War. The *Bedfordshire on Sunday* reported that Mr Rowlett complained his nights were disturbed by locked doors being heard to open and close, mysterious footsteps, and old swing classics such as 'In the Mood' and 'Moonlight Serenade' suddenly piping up on the jukebox when it wasn't turned on. He told locals that everything was always switched off, but he would get into bed, hear voices, and then the music would start. He would not dare go downstairs and swore that Glenn Miller was there.

The Glenn Miller band was quartered in Bedford after coming to England in 1944, and played at several venues in Bedford as well as making recordings there. Miller was forty years old when tragically lost on a flight to France in December that same year.

I end this round-up with the only case I know of an apparently thirsty pub ghost. It comes from the 1950s (via the *Yorkshire Evening Press*) and concerns a public house in South Shields, The Grotto, so-called because it was built from a hewn-out cave in the side of a cliff which was once the abode of a hermit.

'Pride of the pub,' the paper reported, 'is an ancient tankard, said to be several hundred years old. The landlord fills it with beer at night, after closing time, places it on a shelf where no one can reach it without a ladder, and locks both entrances to the bar, drawing iron grilles across the doorways. He swears it is impossible for anyone to get in.

'In the morning the tankard is empty.'

Haunted to the Gallows

William Sheward was a tailor, a meek little man, a bit of a dreamer, and rather too fond of seeing a brighter side to life through a glass of whisky. He was just the careless, moony type of man to fall under the domination and possession of a woman older than himself, and that is what happened. On marrying Julia he found that he had a gaoler as well as a wife.

The marriage of this ill-matched Norwich couple would produce one of the most intriguing murder riddles of the Victorian years, linked to a formidable haunting.

Julia Sheward was described as a frosty-featured woman, excessively houseproud, 'whose chief object was the cultivation of respectability and the more gloomy and monotonous things of life', according to contemporary accounts. She hated children and dogs. Her favourite diversion seemed to be attending funerals, for she seldom failed to be quickly on the scene when one of her friends (apparently she did have some) was on the point of dying. She was bitterly contemptuous of her husband's daydreams and vitriolic about his drinking habits. In short, she cast such a gloom over life that one day he just snapped. In a blind, desperate mental state he stabbed her to death with a large pair of scissors that he used for cutting out cloth in his shop.

Afterwards he sat staring helplessly at the corpse for

some hours. Then, as dawn was breaking, he roused himself, clumsily dismembered the body and buried it at various places in lonely Deepdene Lane, on the outskirts of Norwich.

He told neighbours and customers that Julia had left him, an explanation that drew little surprise for she had openly threatened to walk out on him because she was fed up with his 'drunken, idle ways'. Everyone supposed that the strong-minded Mrs Sheward must have gone back to London, where she once lived, to open up a new way of life for herself.

William Sheward, however, suffered dreadfully within himself. Even in death his wife dominated his thoughts. He could not keep away from the lane in which he had buried her remains; a strong compulsion forced him to the spot whenever he could spare a few minutes. Sometimes, even when busy in his shop, he would suddenly feel the call to revisit the lane.

Before long an alert young police constable noticed how frequently Sheward was attracted to the spot. Why was he, a man without a dog, always poking about in the ditches and undergrowth? Had he lost – perhaps even hidden – something there? Then came another suspicion. The tailor's wife had disappeared quite suddenly; could it possibly be that he had done away with her?

The constable borrowed a bloodhound, and with the animal, beat about the undergrowth at the same spots on which Sheward had bestowed so much attention. The policeman's search was soon rewarded. The dog found a human hand in a ditch. Later, police unearthed a foot, and other parts of a female corpse. But the head of the body was never found.

Things looked bleak for William Sheward as the remains were handed to a local surgeon for a special autopsy and report. The surgeon, after thorough examination, was able to tell the police what the victim was like: 'Age between 26-30, probably light brown hair, weight eight stone. Medium build, good figure. Size four-and-a-half shoes. Clean, well-trimmed nails, and both hands and feet belonging to a person not accustomed to toil or to wear coarse, heavy shoes.'

But Julia Sheward's hair was black. Her weight was nearly ten stone. And she was fifty-six at the time of her disappearance.

The medical report saved Sheward from the hangman and people ready to condemn him quickly changed their attitude. He went on to prosper, acquiring other properties. But in private he remained a haunted man. He could not rid himself of the conviction that Julia, his dead wife, still exercised control over him, paralysing his will, guiding him during his walks, always drawing him back to the lane where he had buried her. Moreover, he lived in constant fear of the police, for he was certain that in spite of the surprisingly misleading medical report, they still suspected he had killed Julia.

One winter's afternoon a large, solid, bowler-hatted man called on William Sheward. He politely introduced himself; he was a detective-inspector. Sheward managed to hide his panic until the detective stated his business. He wanted Mrs Sheward's address and Sheward was the only person likely to know it. 'What was the trouble?' Sheward asked. No trouble, said the inspector. The fact was that a sum of £300 had been left to Mrs Julia Sheward and they could not trace her. If she wanted the money she must appear before a magistrate and claim it.

Saved again. Sheward lightly responded to the effect that if the police could not find the address of his runaway wife then he certainly couldn't. And that was that.

Ten years after the murder William Sheward married again. He married in order not to be alone. The ghost of his first wife haunted him so persistently that he desperately needed human company. The second Mrs Sheward, however, did not take kindly to his habit of waking her in the dead of night and asking her foolish questions; and she liked still less the way he was constantly disturbed by imaginary voices. She also found it peculiar that he could only think of one place to go for a walk, always thrashing about with his walking stick.

Sheward's uneasy ways got on her nerves and there were quarrels. Eventually she suggested it would do them both good to have a change, and she thought they might spend a few days in London. Sheward agreed, and she went ahead and made all the arrangements.

When they arrived at the modest hotel she had booked he looked out at the square and told her he felt there was something wholly odd about the place. Then it came to him. He was actually back in the very London square where, some thirty years ago, he had first met the wife he had murdered. The hotel he was now standing in might have been the house in which Julia had lived as a young girl. If Julia's menacing soul had anything to do with it, this *was* the house.

In a sudden madness, Sheward could see Julia's face gleaming from the fireplace and reflecting from the panes of glass in the old-fashioned bow window. Looking out he saw a policeman slowly pacing along the pavement below. For the second time in his life he snapped. He dashed downstairs, ran out to the officer and made a full confession.

He was executed for the murder of Julia Sheward just eighteen years after he had committed the crime.

The mystery of the highly misleading medical report on the bodily remains discovered in the lane was never resolved; a fire which destroyed official documents has defeated researchers. What the wretched William Sheward saw drove him to the gallows.

Diana's Grandfather

The strange haunting of Diana, Princess of Wales' ancestral home, Althorp House, near Northampton, by the ghost of her grandfather, the seventh Earl Spencer, was kept a family secret for years, until revealed in the 1990s by her brother, Charles.

Diana, Princess of Wales, born Lady Diana Spencer, was fourteen and heartbroken when her grandfather died in June 1975, aged eighty-three. The following year, the old man's ghost was seen at Althorp for the first time.

It happened at a party held to welcome the eighth Earl's new wife and Diana's stepmother, Raine, daughter of novelist Dame Barbara Cartland: five guests were said to have spotted the ghost of the late Earl in the crowd. Later, his phantom figure was seen twice by the butler's wife. She was so startled the first time that she said to it: 'How nice to see you, my lord.'

On another occasion a painter working in the house fled in fright after seeing the late Earl walk past him down a corridor.

The ghostly appearances went on for over two years, until in 1978 Raine decided the sightings were upsetting her ailing husband, who had suffered a stroke, and determined to get rid of the ghost. She believed that her dangerously ill husband was being troubled by the spirit of his father, because of an earlier feud. Accordingly she called in the Rev. Victor Malan, of All Saints' Church, Northampton, in an attempt to clear the sixteenth-century house of its ghost once and for all. Mr Malan conducted a service of blessing, splashing holy water on the walls and saying prayers to ward off the spirit.

His ministration was successful. The ghost vanished, and Diana's father, who had been so close to death, made a good recovery.

But there was a surprising twist. The ghost of the old Earl reappeared fourteen years later, in January 1992. This time a tour guide at Althorp saw 'the ghost of an old man' going up the main staircase. Just weeks later, Diana's father died from a heart attack in hospital, aged sixty-eight. The family remained silent about the strange happenings at Althorp until, months after his father's death, Diana's brother Charles Spencer, the new ninth Earl, told the whole story to *The People* newspaper.

The paper reported that Charles said when his father had his first stroke everything was tried as it was very likely he was going to die. The Church's help had been sought because his grandfather's ghost was seen as a negative force which might have something to do with his father's illness. He was surprised that his stepmother had resorted to anything like that, but it showed she was trying everything and it did put an end to the sightings at that time. There was no thought of using the same ritual when the ghost reappeared, as his father was not then believed to be very ill.

The new Earl said so many down-to-earth people had seen the ghost of his grandfather, particularly in the library and the corridor outside. One was the old housekeeper, a very steady person who had worked at Althorp for years. The late Earl was also seen by a cousin, walking up and down the corridor. People who had seen the ghost said it made the hair stand up on the back of their neck.

In a candid interview given to the *Sunday Telegraph* in 1997, Lord Rees-Mogg, a former editor of *The Times*, told how his family was haunted by a banshee.

He said she had appeared to cousins of his in America, and he himself had seen her in dreams three times. Once the banshee's appearance related to his sister. The second referred to his father, who died nine months later. The last appearance related to his mother, who subsequently had a bad fall. On this last occasion, he said, he snatched the banshee's broomstick and chased her away. She had not been back.

The banshee, Lord Rees-Mogg explained, was basically benign. She helped one to prepare for death. When his father died, Lord Rees-Mogg said he had already been in mourning for nine months.

Living with a Ghost

It was just another ordinary, square-built, Victorian house in Cheltenham, but it was the scene of a particularly sorrowful domestic drama.

The first occupant, on losing his beloved wife, took to drink. When he married again his second wife tried hard to cure him, but unfortunately became a drunkard herself. The hapless couple separated, and within a few months the husband was dead. Two years later the second wife died; but four years after her death her weeping ghost returned to the house where she had experienced so much misery.

At this time a Captain Morton and his large family had come to live in the house. His nineteen-year-old daughter, a medical student, was the first to see the widow's ghost. She testified:

'I had gone up to my room when I heard someone at the door. I saw no one, but on going a few steps along the passage I saw the figure of a tall lady. She was dressed in black of a soft woollen material. A general effect of blackness suggested a bonnet with a long veil.

'The first time I spoke to her she came in past me and walked to the sofa and I asked if I could help. I thought she was going to speak, but she only gave a slight gasp and moved towards the door, disappearing. I also attempted to touch her, but she always eluded me.'

The phantom widow was followed into the garden,

where she stopped when spoken to. A retired general in the neighbouring house saw her crying in the orchard and mistook her for a real person.

Sometimes in the Morton house there were bumps against bedroom doors and the handles turned. A servant was terrified. So was a retriever, while a terrier twice wagged its tail and jumped up at an invisible something, then slunk away.

One member of the family reported: 'It was a fine July evening and I was sitting alone in the drawing room singing, when suddenly I felt a cold, icy shiver and I saw the figure bend over me as if to turn over the pages of my song.'

At least seven people saw the Morton ghost and twenty others heard her. Some felt 'a cold wind' as she passed them. She always turned up unexpectedly, never when the family and friends deliberately kept watch, or when they had been talking or thinking about her.

She continued to be sighted over several years, until gradually becoming less substantial and finally disappearing altogether.

The Morton case caused a minor sensation in the 1880s, provoking much scepticism. Nowadays we know that such hauntings are real enough and occur all too frequently. Many people learn to live with them while they last.

When an old Grade 1 listed mansion house in Devon came up for sale in 1993 *The Daily Telegraph* went along to have a look at it and produced some interesting findings. For Bowden House, near Totnes, was found to have a group of ghosts in residence. They included a little girl in blue; several monks; a grey lady; and a gentleman from Tudor times.

The property was on a site that had been occupied continuously since the Norman Conquest. It had, among other things, a Tudor hall, a Queen Anne hall, a sunken

Italian garden and a medieval jail with guardroom above.

The little girl ghost was known to be Alison Eteson, who was just seven years old when she died of tuberculosis in 1765, during the reign of George III. The ghost of the Tudor gentleman was said to have been seen in the grounds, while spectral monks who chanted in the inner courtyard had been reported from the six holiday-let cottages in the grounds.

The Petersen family, who had owned Bowden House for nearly twenty years, lived more than amicably with their assorted ghosts and were happy to share them with day trippers. Christopher Petersen, son of the owners, and his wife, Belinda, dressed up in period costume to welcome ghost-hunting tourists. Nearly twenty sightings had been reported that year, including two of the wandering Alison, dressed in blue with shoulder-length hair. That was the surprising thing about the Bowden ghosts; all the witnesses described them in colour.

Christopher himself reported that a bright light had travelled up his hand and arm for about ten seconds while he was doing some stonework. He was told that it was a spirit trying to make contact.

My friend Vince Mattocks, the artist, tells me about the ghost his grandmother lived with.

'During the 1970s my grandparents, Reginald and Ethel May Vincent, lived in a block of flats in Weoley Castle, a suburb of Birmingham. When my grandmother went into hospital my grandfather went to stay at their son's, and their daughter – my mother – went to the flat to generally tidy up and change the curtains before Ethel's discharge from hospital. Mother had been to the flat many times, but never on her own before. It was mid-morning and she was changing the curtains when she felt something touch her on the shoulder. Having looked around, she dismissed this as her imagination. Later she again felt something touch her and brush past her. Although she could see nothing she felt quite frightened, so abandoned the curtains and returned home. That evening she went back to the flat with my father, to whom she had told nothing of her uncanny experience, and they put the curtains up without anything unusual happening.

'Ethel returned from hospital and Mother went to visit her. Ethel asked if, when Mother had been to the flat alone, she had sensed anything in the place. Mother said yes, she had been frightened; she thought something touched her and felt she was being watched. Ethel then told her the whole story. She said "the old bloke" who used to live there was still around. She was never frightened of his ghost because she maintained "the dead can't hurt you". The only time it had worried her was when she felt something smothering her while she was in bed.

'Lights used to be on for no reason, doors opened, and objects, such as cushions, were moved around the flat. The coat hangers in the hall used to swing as an unseen presence moved past. My grandfather was generally unaware of these incidents, thinking Ethel had left the lights on herself, and so on.

'Only on one occasion did Ethel ever see the ghost. He was standing in a corner of the room, and she asked him what he wanted. Needless to say, he did not reply!

'Shortly after having seen the ghost my grandmother asked the caretaker about who had lived there before and was told that a couple had been the previous long-term residents. The man had died in hospital and his wife had moved away. No one else had lived there for any length of time until my grandparents moved in. Ethel described the ghost to the caretaker and he said yes, that was the man. She concluded that his lonely ghost had come back to look for his wife.

'Over the years my mother visited several times, though she would never remain in the flat alone. The ghostly activity continued: one day, as Ethel was taking the rubbish to the chute, a pair of shoes were thrown out of the front door behind her.

'After Ethel's own death my grandfather continued living in the flat for about a year, but was untroubled by the eerie occurrences, which seemed to be attracted to women. As far as is known, the ghost could still be there!'

Publisher Jane Tatam had a thoroughly unhappy experience in a house she took at Meonstoke, Hampshire. She told me:

'When I moved in I spent my first night in the back bedroom and woke (or half woke) early to see an old man in an old-fashioned vest, braces and trousers walking across the corner of the room, apparently oblivious to me. Almost dreaming, I went back to sleep, and when I woke, convinced myself it was a dream. I certainly had not felt threatened.

'But in seven years in that house, I felt increasingly uncomfortable and oppressed by it. It somehow felt unlucky. I lost my job within three months of moving in and after that never had a sensible reason for being there, since future jobs were never in the right place. After a series of job losses I felt ever more uneasy and grew to believe that there was a bad presence in the house. I never could sleep there in total darkness, although I've never had that problem before or since.

'About a year before I moved, I decided on a whim to consult a clairvoyant about my future. When I telephoned, I was told that this particular clairvoyant visited one at home. The visit was duly arranged, but within seconds of him arriving (and I had not even thought to mention it) he told me there was 'a very bad presence in the house – violent and possessive'. I took him round the house and asked him to identify any particular spot that seemed worse than any other. He led me straight to the spot where I had seen my 'visitor' on the first night I slept there.

'The clairvoyant suggested that I simply sprinkle the four corners of this room with water left in the sun all day and politely ask the presence to leave. "Do it for a week," he said, "then do the same to all the other rooms on the last night." I did. On the final night of this procedure the brackets of both hanging baskets outside the back door came adrift and bent, and the glass back door shattered. There were rational explanations: the wood round the screws holding the brackets had rotted; a stone from the drive must have hit the door.

'Within a year I finally sold the house that I had been trying to sell for four years. I now sleep in the dark again!'

My correspondent Colin Cake tells me of a house in which he encountered a strange 'frigid zone'. The house, in the Mendips, was originally built as a rectory for the parish church early in the sixteenth century. It was rebuilt and enlarged over the years, and finally modernised when friends of Colin bought it in 1969. It stands on a slight rise, with yew trees on its northern side.

Colin first visited the house in the summer of 1986.

'Coming in from the back and going towards the lounge, I passed an area of intense cold. My hostess noticed me shiver, and with a gentle smile asked me, or rather told me that "I had felt it." I asked where the terrific draught was coming from, and she said there was no draught and prompted me to walk slowly back. I did, and felt this awful drop in temperature again.

'I have done this many times now and it is still the same. It is a small area, about six feet by six feet, and is where the back stairway originally came down to the kitchen and scullery area, no longer there.

'On two occasions when my wife and I have been to a semi-formal dinner with others, I have been standing within this "frigid zone" and about six feet from the others when we have been ready to go into the dining room – and have seemingly been invisible to them!

'Once, in broad daylight, my wife could not find me. Although I was within touching distance of her, she was asking where I was. It was thought I may be out having a "puff"; then one of the others pointed out that I was by one of the yew trees that could be seen through the open front door. Beneath the tree was a man, leaning against the trunk, smoking a pipe. As I moved to see who this was I came out of the cold area, frightening my wife and the others with my sudden appearance.

'The fact that I could not possibly be in two places at the same time prompted investigation as to who was the smoker beyond the door. But, as may be guessed, this "person" was no longer there. It is still a source of wonder to those present as to how I managed to get from the front to the back of the house in zero time. Only the hostess believed me, affirming that I was by her side all the time; the others were convinced that I was carrying out some very involved practical joke.

'Neither my friend nor his wife smoke, and should I be desperate I go out to the garden or to a small outbuilding if the weather is bad. Other smokers do the same. But oddly there have been times when the smell of pipe tobacco, which is easily distinguishable from cigarettes, has been noticed inside the house, and broken clay pipes have been found in the fireplace of the study. Pipe "dottles" have turned up unaccountably in other rooms and spent matches are common.'

Colin had an earlier brush with the uncanny in the open, and in daylight. We have the date, time and place: June 1974, in the city of Bath, about 3 p.m.

'Coming out of one of the shops close to the Abbey, I was approached by someone I thought to be normal. This "man" was dressed in fawn-coloured tight-legged trousers, brown boots with spats, a single-breasted high-buttoned jacket, yellow waistcoat, white shirt with a stiff, rounded collar showing a gold stud, a black, loosely tied bow and a brown, low-domed bowler. He moved directly towards me, holding his left hand out with the palm facing me in a manner that suggested I stop. He then started to speak, but seemed to be struggling to get the words out, opening and closing his mouth rather like a goldfish. After what can only have been a few seconds, I asked him if he was all right. Was he ill? He shook his head. I suggested he sit on one of the seats by the Abbey and looked round for the nearest. When I looked back, there was no one.

'I believe this to be a fairly common sighting.'

We have seen how houses can be haunted by a smell, but the experience of a young Kent family has to be more curious than most. They were haunted not by one smell but by several, and all of them to do with food. Sometimes their semi-detached house near Maidstone was filled with the aroma of fried eggs and bacon, or burnt toast. Also on the ghostly 'menu' were roast beef, stew, sausages and coffee. The smells haunted the whole family: Joan and John Sapsford and their two children. They came at all times of the day and night, and all over the house. Mr Sapsford tried to find out if the house was on the site of an ancient building, which might give a clue to the ghost haunting them in this peculiar way. But he discovered that the only other building on the site had been a gardening nursery. His wife emphasised that the smells did not frighten them, though people thought they were imagining things until they looked in and caught a whiff themselves.

Mediums believe a smell is just one of the ways that spirits can make contact with the living, if a family is sensitive to them.

Much has been written about Elvis Presley in the years since his death, but I doubt if even the most speculative writer would have envisaged him haunting a flat in London. But that is apparently what happened in 1994, when a priest staged a special prayer session to banish the ghost.

It happened at a council flat in Brixton, where a

mother feared that the American rock king, who died in 1977, was haunting her three-year-old son. A neighbour first spotted the ghost while having tea with the boy's mother. When given a pack of Elvis cards to hold, the neighbour started shaking and saw what she thought was Elvis standing across the sitting room. She began screaming and crying, unable to help herself. She could not see the singer's eyes. Then the ghost just changed into a white figure. It lasted for a full two minutes.

Since that first sighting, the mother told *The Sun*, an evil spirit had been tormenting her son. She thought it was trying to lure him into jumping from their second-floor window. So she called in the Rev. Noel Cooper, of All Saints' Church, to deal with the evil influence. Whether it was Presley's ghost or whatever malignant force at work, Mr Cooper said he hoped that the power of God's word would rid the flat of its visions; and presumably, it did.

One of the most poignant stories told to me regarding the ghost of someone returning to a house shortly after death is that of a tragedy that occurred in the aftermath of the Second World War, concerning a German ex-prisoner-of-war in this country.

Mrs Edith Bowden, who was in her fifties, and her younger sister, Mrs Florence Phillipo, both of Whetstone, north London, had befriended the ex-POW whom they knew only as Fritz. Eventually the time came for him to be repatriated, but because his home was in the Russian zone, Fritz became very depressed. Half an hour after leaving Mrs Bowden's house for the last time, he hanged himself in a park.

Three months later, at 6.30 in the morning, Mrs Bowden's husband had just left their bedroom to make a cup of tea when Mrs Bowden heard a voice say: 'Look up.' She raised herself from her pillow and there at the foot of the bed, with arms folded, stood a tall figure in a flowing, slate-grey cloak, grey braided hood, girdle, loose sleeves and monk-like slippers of rope. A moment later it vanished into the wall.

'I was horrified,' Mrs Bowden told me, 'it was the ghost of Fritz. I gasped, "Oh, Glory!" then plunged my head under the bedclothes, my heart thumping violently. I was so shocked I can't say what was the expression on Fritz's face, whether he was sad or smiling, but the sandals on his feet were unmistakably like those Fritz made for himself before he died.

'If ghosts have a purpose, I can only think he came back to try and convey to me that he was sorry he had distressed us and his mother in Germany by hanging himself. I think he wanted my forgiveness.'

The Head of Roger

Of all the haunted homes of the gentry of yesteryear, ancient Wardley Hall, a few miles from Manchester, comes high on the list for its unique, grisly story.

The manor, near Swinton, dates from the sixteenth century. It was built during the short reign of Edward VI, the boy King. A black and white half-timbered building, it was built in quadrangular form, entered by a covered archway opening into a courtyard in the centre. It was originally protected by a moat on three sides.

For its first hundred years the manor was occupied uneventfully. It was then taken over by the Downe family. By the mid-seventeenth century the master there was a grandson, Roger Downe, the last male representative of an old, respected family. He turned out to be its black sheep. He was reputedly one of the most licentious courtiers at the court of Charles II, the Merry Monarch.

Roger Downe spent the greater part of his dissolute life in London and was rarely at home. His sister, Maria, and her devoted cousin, Eleanor, led a quiet, secluded life with the family's servants at Wardley Hall.

One day in London, Roger molested a girl and ran his sword through a man who came to defend her. He was acquitted of murder, but some time later was himself slain in a drunken brawl or riot on London Bridge. In the mêlée a watchman made a stroke at him with his bill or halberd and severed Roger's head from his body.

Roger had not been home to Wardley Hall for a considerable time and his sister and her companion had started to worry about him. Late one night, as they were making ready for bed, a delivery cart arrived at the mansion.

A manservant brought in a rough wooden box, the lid securely fastened with nails and the whole bound with twine. The box, the servant announced, had been sent from London and delivered by the usual Manchester carrier. The address label bore Maria Downe's name and was written in a rough handwriting which she did not recognise. There seemed to be something unsettling, something sinister, about the mysterious box. The two women were in no hurry to have it opened. They went to bed. But later, Maria rang for a servant to bring the box up to her room. Still reluctant to finish opening it, the initial work having been done by the servant, she decided to leave it till the morning. But she spent a very disturbed night, the box seeming to exert a strange influence on her dreams. As dawn broke, she could delay her curiosity no more and opened it.

What she found to her horror was a human head, the hair unkempt and matted and the features bruised and bloody, yet not so disfigured that she could not recognise the head of her own brother. She fainted, to be found by a maid lying there in shock.

When Maria had recovered her battered senses she ordered the box, closed and rebound with twine, to be taken to an outhouse. The retainer who unwittingly carried it there was stunned when, on setting it down, 'a deliberate knock, dull but clear, issued from it, and was repeated in a manner as might be made by an impatient visitor when anxious to gain admission. The man's hair stood on end and running into the Hall he blurted out to his fellow servants that the Evil One had come and was lying in the stables in "yon cursed box".'

This caused consternation among the servants, none of whom dared to venture near the building which housed the terrible and mysterious box. They now regarded their mistress, the recipient of it, with awe.

The next piece of evidence comes from another servant who told what he saw one morning in the grey light of dawn. He slept with his window open. Awakened by footsteps in the courtyard below, he got up to see who was moving about at such an early hour. To his surprise he saw flitting across the yard a woman bearing a lantern. It was the mistress, Maria. She made for the building housing the box and went inside, reappearing after a time carrying a bulky object under her cloak. The watcher had no doubt what it was. He pulled on a coat and went down into the courtyard. Maria had vanished but he heard sounds in the garden and on looking over a hedge saw her hurriedly digging a large hole into which she deposited the box and rapidly shovelled back the earth.

But Roger's head refused to stay buried. It made such noises, caused such a disturbance, that it had to be hastily dug up and restored to the house. Now the affair becomes a little cloudy, with no more written evidence, only hearsay and legend. But it is fairly well established that whenever other attempts were made to dispose of the head, which eventually of course, became just a skull, it gave off frightful noises and screams, and always in some manner managed to find its way back into the house again, whether with human assistance or of its own ghoulish accord. And there in the house it was found, much later, by investigators.

Maria Downe never discovered who had vengefully sent her the head of her rake of a brother. She was the last of the family. She rejected all suitors and died a spinster, the Hall after her death passing into other hands. This was early in the eighteenth century.

In the 1790s, some one hundred and thirty years after

the ghastly night when Roger's head was delivered, Thomas Barritt, a Manchester antiquary, paid a special visit to Wardley Hall accompanied by three friends. He had heard about a human skull which the occupiers did not dare allow to be removed from its position at the topmost step of a staircase. It was believed that, if removed or ill-used, some uncommon noise and disturbance always followed, to the terror of the household.

Barritt and his companions found the skull bleached white from weather beating on it from a four-square window in the hall, which the occupiers never allowed to be glazed or filled up, believing that the skull became unruly and disturbed if ever the hole was not left open.

Unfortunately, at the end of their visit the last of Barritt's companions to examine the skull neglected to return it to its usual place on the staircase, putting it down instead in the darkened part of a room.

'... The night but one following,' Barritt wrote, 'such a storm arose about the house, of wind and lightning, as tore down some trees, and unthatched out-housing. We hearing of this, my father went over in a few days after to see his mother, who lived near the Hall, and was witness to the wreck the storm had made. Yet all this might have happened had the skull never been removed; but, withal, it keeps alive the credibility of its believers.'

A matter of record was an earlier violent storm that arose when a new maid, thinking the skull was that of an animal, threw it into the moat. After a tempestuous night it was hastily retrieved and put back in its place.

Wardley Hall had a succession of tenants after the Downes. By about 1830 the mansion was badly in need of attention, one part being occupied as a farmhouse and the other formed into a cluster of cottages. However, it was taken over by a wealthy colliery owner who carefully restored it to much of its former glory. All through these times Roger's skull remained firmly in residence.

Around the 1850s a writer who visited the Hall noted

that a door, always locked, had been fitted across the aperture where the skull rested. Two keys were held, one in possession of the tenant and the other kept by the Countess of Ellesmere, who owned the freehold of the property. Occasionally the Countess, armed with her key, would take friends visiting her at neighbouring Worsley Hall over to Wardley Hall to see the now legendary 'screaming skull' that refused to leave home.

In 1930 Wardley Hall was taken over by the Diocese of Salford to become the official residence of the Roman Catholic Bishop of Salford. So it has remained, although its surrounds have changed. Scores of lovely trees in the grounds were demolished to make way for an extension to a motorway. Wardley Hall lost its rather creepy, spooky look in the process.

In recent years a revival of interest in the skull produced a statement that the Bishop of Salford declined to re-open the controversy about it. A member of his household confirmed that the skull was back in its old place in a glass case on the oak staircase but said there was no longer any fear or superstition about it and nothing untoward had happened in the house since the Second World War.

Roger Downe was quiet at last.

Phantoms of the Roads

It was after midnight on a January day in 1996 when a van driving past Witton Cemetery, Birmingham, ran into a man.

The shocked driver, a young plumber, made an emergency stop and quickly got out to search the road, fearful of what he might find. But, puzzlingly, he found no victim and no damage to his van. Yet the man had appeared slap in front of him and he knew he had definitely hit something. Still very worried, he called the police.

It was then he received his second shock. Oh, they told him, he must have seen a ghost. It was not the first time that someone had reported 'bumping into one' in that area.

Such encounters with ghosts of the highways are a regular occurrence, as police records throughout the country can testify. What is not known is the number of drivers who fail to report such unnerving incidents, either refusing to believe the evidence of their own eyes or thinking they must have been the victim of a hallucination. For many drivers alone in a vehicle without witnesses, even more worrying than the initial shock can be the stressful business of having to explain what they saw, what they *know* they saw, to doubters.

But they do happen all the time, these strange and often chilling encounters on the roads. They occur not only at well-known accident blackspots, at places with a sinister reputation or in the wake of suicide or murder, but often without any explanation at all.

From the sound of hoofbeats in the night where there are no horses, to phantom vehicles and figures flying at the windscreen, these uncanny events do at times have an extra witness, sometimes several.

It may be that Black Toby, the Suffolk terror, no longer haunts the Blythburgh Road with his hearse and four headless horses; that his contemporary, the wicked squire over Reydon Hall way, has given up haunting the Wangford-Reydon Road with his phantom coach and four; and that the ghostly coach and six driven by a headless driver goes dashing down the hill at Long Compton, in Warwickshire, no more. But some legendary ghosts do persist in turning up when least expected.

Like the spectral white lady of Samlesbury, in Lancashire. Young Lady Dorothy Southworth has searched for centuries for her lost lover, who was brutally murdered by her own brother. She was last seen in the 1970s. A couple were driving along the main road from Blackburn to Preston, passing within a few feet of fourteenth-century Samlesbury Hall, when the wife saw a young girl cross the road and start running in the direction of Preston. She had on a long, elaborate white dress, and a short cloak over her shoulders and head.

The wife said to her husband: 'You might have stopped and given that poor girl a lift.' He looked puzzled, for he had seen no one.

As other examples of what can happen on the road, let us take two widely differing cases with some fifty years between them.

The first strange story comes from 1924. It became known as the Tall Man of Brook.

On a Sunday evening in May three cyclists, Betty Bone, her brother, Alf, and his friend, Ewart Pope, were riding through the New Forest. It was still light as they reached the Bramshore golf links just beyond the Bell Inn at Brook, where they passed a strange pedestrian at least seven feet tall.

He was dressed in an antique top hat and a long tailcoat. As he was facing the same direction, none of them noticed his face. A quarter of a mile further on, to their great surprise, they saw the Tall Man in front of them again at the top of Telegraph Hill. As before, they did not notice him until they were within twenty paces; he just 'appeared' as if by magic.

Passing him, the three cyclists experienced what they later described as 'a distinct sensation of the eerie, the uncanny'.

At the crossroads of the B3078 with the Fritham to Normansland Road, the man again appeared yet again about twenty paces ahead. By now thoroughly unnerved, the trio pedalled past him furiously, intent on getting as far away as possible. He was never seen again.

Now to a night in October 1976, and the alarming experience of a middle-aged couple driving along the sea front at Seaford, Sussex.

Gordon Cooper and his wife, Iris, were driving home from a house-warming party when they saw a car hurtling towards them with headlights blazing. Mr Cooper slammed on his brakes, but to their horror the other car swerved off the road and plunged through a wall into the sea. The couple both got out and ran to the wall, but were astonished to find it intact, and there was no sign of the other car or driver.

Mr Cooper reported what had happened to the police. They told him that in 1935 a car had crashed into the sea and the driver's body was never recovered. Two years later another car and its driver were swept out to sea after leaving the road. And in 1929, another man was killed when his car crashed near the spot.

Mr Cooper told me: 'I'd only had a couple of beers at the party and my wife some shandy. We saw the car for six or eight seconds. We stopped and wound down the windows. We both saw the same thing. It shook us because there wasn't a trace of anything – we both asked each other where he'd gone.

'We can only think it must have been some ghostly re-enactment of an accident years ago.'

While on this subject I should add what a friend who lives in Oxfordshire wrote to me.

'I had your new ghost book in my hand this morning when the milkman knocked at the front door. When he noticed the book I asked him casually if he believed in ghosts. I was surprised when he said at once, "Yes!" He then told me that he and two friends were driving home one night when they saw a policeman riding a bicycle in front of them. They slowed down, approaching the officer cautiously, but on reaching "him" – no policeman!'

These things do happen. All the time.

Margaret and Joe

Margaret and Joe Ripley decided they might sleep better if their twin beds were shifted round so that they both faced the east. It took a great deal of manoeuvring in the small bedroom they were in at the time, but they managed it. Next thing they knew Joe was up in the night trying to rescue the bedclothes from an entity intent on pulling them off him. It sat invisibly but solidly on the bed, persisting in a fierce tug-o'-war.

Next morning the Ripleys faced the hassle of returning the beds to their original position, so that they might enjoy a peaceful night; but they laughed at the incident then and still do – the very idea that they, a medium and her husband, should themselves be haunted in their own bedroom. Margaret soon found the culprit to be the spirit of a previous occupant, an old lady, who objected to the furniture being moved around.

The Ripleys are unusual in that they work together. Margaret Helena is a medium and clairvoyant. Joe, who comes from a Romany family, also possesses psychic qualities but does not practise, concentrating instead on supporting his wife in her work. Being always in and out of sickness has given Joe a special empathy in helping to deal with people's problems, and these problems do loom large at times. Detecting and clearing a ghost can be only part of the job; often Margaret finds herself having to be a combination of medium, counsellor, social helper and friend.

The couple, both born and bred in Hastings and married nearly fifty years, have dealt with innumerable hauntings, ranging from a simple ghostly presence to the most distressing of cases resulting from indulgence in drugs and black magic.

There was the council house in a Sussex village whose several ghosts forced the frightened family to move out. One of the young children repeatedly saw a woman who wanted him to get out of bed and play with her. She threatened to hang him from a hook. Because the council was unable to rehouse the family they had to flee to private rented accommodation.

Margaret, when called in, found a dreadful atmosphere existing in the pre-war house. She sensed that there had been two suicides, a drowning, and the deaths of two children. She found the child's bedroom to be haunted by a bedridden elderly woman who had once lain there helpless and incontinent. Also, a younger woman who had committed suicide kept coming back to the same bedroom to look for her own children, while the bathroom was visited by a male ghost. Down in the living room lingered the spirit of a young woman who had once 'entertained' troops in the house.

After Margaret had freed its several earthbound spirits the house, which had always been freezing cold, became warm and livable-in again. In the majority of cases, having detected and obtained contact with a ghostly entity, Margaret brings a silent prayer into play to turn the entity round to face the golden light that beckons it. She explains to them that they are not here any more and that their loved ones in the spirit world are waiting for them to return to them. As she communicates with them and offers up her prayer, she gradually sees them going up towards the light and she knows they have gone.

She always takes holy water with her on her visits,

using it to sprinkle and bless a haunted premises and to clear it of any lingering evil.

Margaret firmly believes in the progression of life, in reincarnation. Both her mother and her grandmother were psychic and she herself became aware of her powers as a teenager, when she started 'seeing faces and things'. She trained for ten years to be a medium. More than any of her countless cases of 'ghostbusting' she remembers with both humility and pride the night when, 'as a fledgling', she stood nervously on the rostrum in a full church and received no fewer than seventeen messages from the spirit world.

She works quietly and honestly to her own strict code. If a person is in need of more help than she feels she can give them, she will send them to someone else. She never advertises. All her work is the result of recommendation or, as she puts it, 'word of mouth'. In her capacity as a clairvoyant, she often gets letters and phone calls asking for a reading. A call from Australia. A call from Iceland. A call from anywhere.

There are many things that Margaret can detect and foretell, but there are some things her code will not allow her to divulge. There is one in particular. She has often seen it quite clearly, as later events have always proved, but she would never forewarn that anyone was going to die.

Unfortunately, but perhaps inevitably, the Ripleys have found many hauntings to be the result of suicide. 'We find that people pick up the spirits of those who hanged themselves,' Joe says. 'We go into a room and it feels all icy, all cold, and we know.'

When called to a house in Camber they spotted the trouble even before entering. It was Joe who 'picked up' the thing, whatever it was, outside a window. He pointed and told Margaret: 'There it is – up in that room.' And so it proved. The owner of the house said that was exactly where the trouble was, in a little boy's bedroom. This was a particularly unpleasant case for Margaret, for she had to clear the evil remains of black magic after detecting the sickening activities of a coven that had once practised there.

Not all of Margaret's cases involve ghosts of the dead. One of her worst hauntings was caused by a virulently potent evil being projected by a living person.

A young mother in Brighton was in despair. She had been having a lot of trouble with a dark, frightening atmosphere in her house. She had a new baby and it was affected too, permanently crying, night and day. Although Brighton was outside her area, Margaret agreed to visit the woman when told that others had declined to help her.

The house, it turned out, was a beautiful home on a new estate. The distressed woman, who was in her thirties, said she was on her own because she had had a lot of trouble with her husband, who was now in prison. She met Margaret in the lounge and wanted to describe the atmosphere there, but Margaret told her not to say any more, explaining that she would have to go over the whole property, as the trouble was not always confined to one room.

'We went up this lovely staircase and into the room the woman was sleeping in, but there was nothing there. We then went into the children's room. The mother told us that she had three other children, two girls and a boy, who had been taken into care. There was nothing in this room, either, it was just untidy as a child's room would be. Then we went into the main bedroom, which had been the husband and wife's room, and I came upon the source of the trouble.

'I got penetrating eyes looking into the room. And then I got the person and I knew what it was and also the trouble that this man – the husband – had meted out to his wife.

'We returned downstairs and I was able to tell the wife that her husband, from his cell in prison, was putting his thoughts into that bedroom; it could be done, and they were evil thoughts. He was also projecting them into the lounge; he knew she was in there. He had done the same in the living room, which was why she had had to get out of there. She could not go back into the marriage room so had put herself down in the lounge, but he was now concentrating his evil thoughts in there. I told her I detected he had done some devious things and she confirmed this. I described him to her exactly, although I had never seen him. I also correctly described his mother, who I "saw" lived in a house not far away and emanated evil like her son.'

Margaret told the woman that she had no alternative but to move – and not let anyone know she was moving. She must seek the support of her parents, who would be willing to help. Margaret also advised her on how to go about convincing the authorities that she could care for her other children, and how to get legal help to obtain a divorce. She finally told the wife, 'We have a healing list and we will pray for you.'

A whole year went by and Margaret and Joe heard no more. Then they got a call at Christmas. It was the wife, to say all that Margaret had told her and advised her had come true. Her parents had helped her to find a new home near her mother, she had her children back, and her divorce from her evil partner was going through.

'It was the best Christmas gift we ever had,' Margaret says.

There are not too many lighter moments in Margaret and Joe's activities, but they still smile at the time they were babysitting for their daughter in her house and a couple of ghosts just walked in. Margaret looked up to see a strange woman go through into the kitchen, then walk back out again. Then a man walked in and did the same thing. Joe saw him too. They were the harmless spirits of people who had once lived in the old sea-front property. There is a sequel to this. Margaret and Joe did not tell their daughter what they had seen, but shortly afterwards she told them that she had seen a strange woman 'just sitting there'. From her description it was the very same ghost, who obviously felt quite happy there.

How can anyone looking for a new home make reasonably certain there is nothing 'funny' about it? Margaret has this simple advice:

'When viewing a property, people normally go on a bright day. I say, go on an ordinary day. When you go into the house the first thing you should do is go into every room on your own. If you feel good about it, fair enough, but I do mean *every* room. Say to yourself, "I'm going to live here," and see how you feel about it.'

Goosed by a Ghost

An odd case came to me from the Catherinewheel Hotel at Egham, Surrey, where landlord George Shonk and his wife were given some sleepless nights by two sexy ghosts.

The apparition that flitted into George's room was a blonde in a white negligée. His wife, Patricia, was haunted by the figure of a tall, handsome man.

George told me he thought the ghosts must be looking for each other, but he wished they would hurry up about it so that he and his wife could get some sleep. There was a story of a ghost called Maude who was said to haunt the hotel, but there was no mention of a man.

Ghosts that come under the description of 'sexy spooks' often rate a paragraph in the newspapers, and the 1990s produced a crop of them.

The *Independent on Sunday* reported the case of a ghost of a former landlord of a village pub who had returned to haunt the present licensee and his wife. It was a ghost described as suffering from 'wandering-hand' disease, for landlord Howard Baines, his wife, Trudy, and a cellarman had all been 'goosed' by it. It only attacked staff at the Bird in Hand at Westhay, Somerset, never customers, and seemed to be particularly fond of the landlord and his wife. Mrs Baines had felt fingers running through her hair and cold air on her neck. The trouble was most acute down in the cellar, when they bent over at work. Mr Baines said the ghost only gave a gentle tweak, but it was chilling. He found it funny, but his wife got angry with it sometimes. They were trying to find out the former landlord's name, so they could talk to him. Apparently, in 1865 the pub's then landlord had died in a fire after falling asleep with a glass of cider and a cigar in his hand. He seemed to have been aroused when the Baineses knocked down a wall while refurbishing: it was then that the ghostly incidents began, with glasses flying around the bar and a mirror sent crashing to the floor.

The ghost of a former landlord was also thought responsible for saucy behaviour at a Bradford pub, as *The Daily Telegraph* reported. Young barmaid Susan Hagyard, at the Harp of Erin, complained of being goosed by a ghost that eerily groped her bottom as she pulled pints. She said she often felt a hand touching her and turned round thinking it was a customer who had had one too many, only to find no one there.

It was the latest in a series of ghostly incidents at the one hundred-year-old pub, which had a reputation for being haunted. Colleagues of Susan's had reported a clanking in the cellar. Again, no one was found. Glasses had dropped from the shelves, ornamental plates had leapt off walls and shattered, and the jukebox had gone on the blink. The ghost had also appeared in the room occupied by the landlady – Susan's mother, Joan – and it was she who thought it might be the ghost of a previous landlord up to his tricks.

More alarming was a ghost reported to have attacked a young couple in an ancient Leicestershire pub. It happened in the bar of the Belper Arms, near Measham. The aggressive spirit first groped the girl, who screamed and dropped her drink. No one was near her. It then tried to strangle her boyfriend as he came over to her: he started to choke and grab at his throat. Then the pressure relaxed.

Landlord Douglas Plumb said something similar had

happened before. The ghost was believed to be that of a highwayman who chased women but hated men.

The ghostly culprit making advances at another pub, in Somerset, was believed to be of all people, a nun. Male customers at the Friendly Spirit, Cannington, were reported to have felt their private parts being 'brushed' in the room where Maude de Merriette's remains were bricked up. Maude was stoned to death in the fourteenth century for seducing a monk.

The same ghost also disturbed a barmaid in bed with her boyfriend.

A frightened woman cleaner quit her job at a bingo hall after a ghost there tried to grope her. *The Sun* reported this haunting at the hall in Wednesbury, Staffordshire. The cleaner, a mother-of-three in her forties, was mopping out the ladies' loo when she felt someone behind her touch her on the shoulder, as if seeking to grab her for a quick cuddle. She turned and was shocked to see the spectre of an old man. She screamed, threw her mop and bucket at the figure and ran.

The hall manager admitted it was not the first sighting of the mischievous ghost, nicknamed Fred. Other workers said it sometimes played the one-arm bandits. One saw three bells mysteriously appear in a line and cash pour out, but no one was there. Then there was the bingo caller who heard strange voices and was so scared he locked himself in a cupboard. The ghost also crept up behind a terrified barmaid and put its arms around her.

The hall was formerly a picture house and an old doorman named Fred was known to have died there. It seemed to be his ghost that was still prowling around the place.

A young couple had the fright of their life on honeymoon at a Lancashire hotel. They were lying in bed in the bridal suite when they heard a low moaning, followed by a bumping sound. Then a shape appeared beside the bed in the darkness, like the top half of a man.

The scared couple hurriedly got up and left the room, spending the rest of the night down in the hotel lounge.

They called off their honeymoon and went home. The owner of the hotel, at Poulton-le-Fylde, had never seen the ghost, but the couple learned that it had been sighted a few times and usually had the appearance of a vicar, though they had been far too shocked to notice if the figure had worn a clerical collar. Apparently the hotel had been a vicarage years ago.

The Sun also found a distraught couple who were driven to pursue their love life in a tent in the back garden because of a groaning ghost that haunted their bedroom. They never actually saw the intrusive spirit but they heard and sensed him well enough, and there was a sweet smell whenever he was around. Every time they attempted to cuddle up he started moaning and banging.

A medium told the couple that the ghost was that of a crotchety deep-sea diver who was annoyed by the noise made by their three small children and wanted to stop them having any more.

The husband said that apparently a previous occupant of the house, at Broadstairs, Kent, was in the navy and his friend was a diver. But whoever the ghost was he was certainly very off-putting. There was no way he and his wife could get together in the house, it was like trying to make love in front of a disapproving stranger, so they pitched a tent in the garden. The children, who knew nothing about the ghost, were asleep when they put the tent up, and by the time the children were up they were back inside and the tent was down. The wife said she was convinced the ghost did not want them to have more children. It only turned up when she and her husband were in bed, and was a real passion-killer!

Lastly, an illustration that these kind of ghosts have no respect for the law. A policewoman, in bed in her room in police lodgings, awoke terrified to find a ghost sitting on top of her. At first unable to move, she finally managed to struggle free and ran from the room, understandably refusing to return.

It was not the first ghostly incident at the lodgings, situated behind Putney police station in London. Other officers had reported furniture moving around in empty rooms. The house manager said that beds had been shaken violently with nobody in them and there had been sightings of spirits. The trouble was believed to emanate from a neighbouring graveyard, hundreds of years old. A lot of tough men and women lived at the lodgings but were truly unsettled by the ghostly activity.

A priest visited the building and said prayers in an attempt to get the ghostly entities to leave. As the place was being renovated it was also hoped that the paint smells might help to drive them away.

Join My Ghost Walk

A phenomenon of recent years has been the rise in the number of 'ghost walks'. Towns and cities throughout the country now have these conducted tours of local haunted places and properties.

Many are listed in official tourist information. Some are so well organised as to employ experienced guides and members of Equity, the actors' union, to ensure a lively outing. The walks may be enlivened by the sudden appearance over a wall of a 'ghostly' monk or witch, or something horrible lurching out of a darkened doorway; the leader of the walk may be suitably garbed, perhaps as a Victorian undertaker. All good fun. But at the heart of most of these ghost walks are some well-authenticated hauntings.

In York, where I was competitively offered the choice of two (or was it three?) ghostly tours showing the dark, mysterious side to the ancient city, the attractions ranged from a pile of discarded Roman coffins to the house where 'little Sarah' was walled up alive by the neighbours when her family died of the plague. Sarah died of starvation, looking out of a window on the world from which she was barred. 'There,' says the guide dramatically, 'is the window …'

But in York they also have one of the most remarkable ghost sightings on record.

The Treasurer's House, in the close of York Minster, might seem like something out of the Middle Ages, but in fact the interior of this National Trust property was greatly altered in Edwardian times by the construction of a medieval hall and Georgian drawing rooms by its then wealthy owner. Workmen had to dig deep into the original foundations during this refurbishment.

Some fifty years later, in 1953, a young plumber named Harry Martindale, eighteen years old, was busy down in the cellars installing central heating. He was on a ladder, working at a wall. There were no windows down there and the only lighting was what he had brought with him.

As he worked away he heard what he thought at first was the sound of a car horn, but he was too deep underground and the note was held too long for it to be that. Then, to his astonishment, a man walked through the wall, a perfectly solid man, while above him appeared a second man on a horse, blowing on the horn. Martindale, who had fallen from his ladder, could now hear sounds of movement, and he watched in amazement as the two passed across the cellar, followed by some twenty other helmeted men, all walking into the opposite wall. The whole thing was over in seconds. Martindale was seized by the fear that one of the men might turn and look at him, but no one did. He was found an hour later by the house curator, still sitting on the cellar floor and in such a state that he was sent home. He was off work for two weeks, treated for shock by a doctor. He never went back to his job and later became a policeman.

What was it he had seen? From the young man's description, experts identified the ghostly troop as a platoon of Roman soldiers; a rather scruffy lot, unlike the Technicolor variety usually seen in the movies, which was why Martindale had not recognised them. Then there was his observation that, strangely, they all seemed to be cut off at the knees, as if they were walking in the floor. Later excavation supplied the answer. It was discovered that the

Roman road from legionary headquarters to the north-east gate, once thought to be under the modern street, was actually under the Treasurer's House... two feet below the cellar floor. So no wonder the ghosts the young plumber had seen had been cut off at the knees – they had been walking on the surface of the old road.

Harry Martindale's uncanny experience that day, down in the Treasurer's House cellar, remains one of the most fascinating ghost sightings of the twentieth century.

At that other splendid Roman city, Chester, one of the most exhilarating experiences, steeped in history and adventure, used to be a walk all the way round the city walls. It still is, but now there is also the inevitable ghost walk. Chester claims to have more ghosts than any other city in Britain. They include phantom monks and a headless Saxon who haunts a car park. There is also to be seen, in church ruins, the coffin of a monk who committed murder and was buried vertically in the wall; while standing out amid all the horrors is God's Providence House on Watergate Street, the only house in town to escape the fourteenth-century Black Death. In London, the operators of Jack the Ripper tours, following the murderer's ghastly trail, now vie for customers with ghost walks offering a dramatic tour of back streets and hidden haunts.

In Edinburgh one is offered a ghosts and witches walk through the Old Town and Royal Mile, the many attractions including no fewer than four apparitions said to appear in Charlotte Square. It was here in this city in the eighteenth century that members of the Edinburgh Hellfire Club (Satan worshippers) used to meet. During one meeting, the devil appeared and all present went insane.

Back to the Roman cities. Bath, with all it has to offer from that ancient world, also has its tour of haunted houses. So does Exeter, although here the ghost walk has more to do with the grave. From Roman times until the seventeenth century, the Cathedral Green at Exeter was one vast cemetery, with bodies resting up to ten deep – about a quarter of a million of them, all told. On to Victorian times and the dreadful practice of body-snatching, which brought about the building of protective catacombs; a visit to them can be included in the tour. In all this sombre history there are some ghosts with a less stifling air about them. Like the Duchess of Clarence, who is sometimes to be seen at a window of the Royal Clarence Hotel, dressed in all her splendour.

A ghost walk in the Old Town of Hastings, nestling close by the sea, features the ghosts of smugglers too. There are tales – and plenty of evidence – of secret tunnels everywhere, even from house to house, when smuggling was rife. The ghost of the most notorious smuggler, however, is said to haunt a spot a little farther up the coast. He is Toby Rawlings, an eighteenth-century sailor and smuggler who was murdered in an isolated cove at Fairlight Glen. His aggrieved spirit is believed to walk about there still.

Back in the Old Town we can take a look at the haunting histories of two splendid black-timbered medieval houses, both situated in quaint and narrow All Saints' Street and both dating from the fifteenth century.

First, 'Shovells'. This house with its nodding upper storey is reputed to have been the home of the mother of Admiral Sir Cloudesley Shovell, back in the seventeenth century. A painted sign showing the bewigged Admiral in his prime hangs outside. Shovells has a narrow smugglers' passage between two of the bedrooms and is connected with one of the original parish churches. It was once used as a paupers' home. It is also haunted. The ghost of a lady in black, possibly a previous owner, has been seen there several times in recent years. Whether the Shovells, mother and son, ever returned to the house in spirit is not known, though they had more cause than most to vent their ghostly spleen.

Cloudesley Shovell, who went to sea at fourteen, forged a fine naval career for himself, only for it to end in utter disaster. On 22 October 1707 the Admiral was returning with a fleet of fifteen ships from action in the Mediterranean. They had sunk eight French ships and were in high spirits, having left Toulon after a fabulous celebration party. But on this day, a combination of bad navigation and bad weather drove Shovell's fleet on to rocks off the Scilly Isles. The fifty-seven-year-old Admiral's flagship, the *Association*, went down with the horrific loss of eight hundred officers and men, Shovell's two sons among them. Three other ships were sunk, the rest escaping with great difficulty. Shovell's body was found washed ashore at Port Hellick Cove, on the island of St Mary's. He was buried at Westminster Abbey.

The gruesome twist to this sea tragedy came thirty years later, when a woman on the Scillies confessed on her death-bed to having been the first to find Shovell in the cove, lying there more dead than alive. Coveting an emerald ring on one of his fingers, she 'extinguished the flickering life' of the Admiral and took it.

The dying woman produced the ring to the clergyman who heard her startling confession.

From stark tragedy to the heart-warming story of our second haunted house in All Saints' Street, which came into the news in the 1990s.

Professor John Povey and his wife, Gail, from California, fell in love with the old timbered house on a visit to the Old Town, and in the 1970s he bought it. The professor was Dean at the University of California, specialising in English literature. He and his wife lived at the Old Town house on summer holidays and whenever they could on his travels. The professor developed a great fondness for the Old Town and when he died from cancer in 1992 it was his dying wish that the house, when disposed of, should go to help the community. His widow, in America, duly pledged the proceeds of the sale to the parish of St Clement and All Saints, in gratitude for the happy times she and her husband had spent there. It was decided the money would go to the churches' restoration fund.

And the ghost? Also a happy and harmless resident, as the late professor's sister, Mrs Gladys Hutcheson, explained to the local paper. It was a friendly spirit, she said, which she liked to call the Old Man. She recalled that the first time she visited the house her dog would only sit in the fireplace. When she took him to an upstairs room he ran around the walls until she went back downstairs. On another night she awoke to hear breathing. She thought it was her dog, until she realised she did not have the animal with her. Then there was the friend who was staying who thought she heard her walking around the room ...

But, Mrs Hutcheson said, it was a wonderful house with a friendly atmosphere, and the happiness of the professor and his wife during their stay there marked their gift to the Christian community.

Before leaving All Saints' Street I should record the experience there of a professional photographer friend of ours. A few years ago workmen were busy restoring another very old house. Our friend, who was taking pictures, stepped back in the narrow street to allow a man and his dog to go by, then resumed her work.

The puzzled builder said, 'What did you step back for?'

She told him – to let the man and his dog go by.

'There wasn't a man and his dog here,' the builder said stoutly. 'But there was in the fifteenth century.'

However, our friend knew what she had seen.

She Walks the Castle

It was just prior to the start of the First World War. Little Mabel Cole, daughter of the licensee of the Fortune of War public house in Priory Road, Hastings, enjoyed playing with young friends near the entrance to Hastings Castle. One night Mabel, aged ten, had a strange, vivid dream in which six nuns appeared, carrying a coffin down the pathway from the entrance to the castle.

In time she forgot the dream. But in the 1950s, more than forty years afterwards, something happened that brought her memory of that night flooding back. Two young nurses from New Zealand visiting the castle ruins stopped to take a snapshot, one of the other. When the picture was developed they were staggered to see on it the image of a nun appearing over the shoulder of the girl being photographed.

Legend has it that a nun at the castle had a baby and was put to death. The ghost of a grey nun has been seen by many people over the years, often carrying a bundle, believed to be a baby. She generally walks on a high bank of grass close to the western portion of the curtain wall, which ends abruptly where the cliff has fallen away.

Mabel Cole's brother, Les, who has lived most of his life in a house immediately below the castle walls, told me that many a time when tending his garden he has had the uneasy feeling of his every move being followed by silent watchers in the empty ruins above. There have been numerous uncanny incidents recently, such as the day a gardener working in the castle grounds came to him, very shaken, and asked: 'Do you believe in ghosts?' He took Mr Cole to a part of the castle site and told him, 'I was standing here – when I saw somebody disappear into that hedge over there!' There was no way it could have been a human body on that steep, wired-off spot.

There is not much of the lofty cliff-top castle remaining these days, just some walls and the odd archway, but it retains a special place in history. It was here that the invading William the Conqueror raised a high mound of earth and sand and erected on it one of several prefabricated wooden forts he brought over from Normandy in his invasion fleet. He then went off to fight and win the Battle of Hastings.

One of William's first orders as King of England was that his wooden fortress at Hastings should be splendidly rebuilt in stone. It was the very first of the Norman castles (they went on to build some two hundred others), and in its thriving days kings stayed there. There have been other reports of ghostly activity at the ruins, including the apparition of a Victorian lady, and a wandering woman in white who committed suicide. There have also been suspected phenomena down in the storage cellars or dungeons, hewn out of rock, which were only rediscovered in the 1870s. But the most fascinating ghost on record has to be that of the castle itself. Fishermen at sea off Hastings in the early hours have reported seeing the strange and wonderful sight of the ruins transformed and Hastings Castle standing proudly aloft in all its glory of nearly a thousand years ago.

A few miles west along the coast from Hastings lies Pevensey, where the invading William of Normandy actually landed, and here he found the ample remains of a vast castle built hundreds of years earlier by the conquering Romans. Inside its massive outer walls William erected another of his prefabricated wooden forts, later building a proper keep. Parts of the castle's towers, dungeons, keep and chapel remain today.

There have been reports of ghostly Romans being seen at and around Pevensey Castle. Strangely, never a Norman. There are other ghosts, including an unknown 'Spanish lady', last seen in the 1960s. But the most prominent, and seemingly resident ghost is that of a very courageous woman.

In 1399, a turbulent time when Henry, Duke of Lancaster, sought to wrest the crown from Richard II (and succeeded, becoming Henry IV), the Constable at Pevensey Castle, Sir John Pelham, went off to fight alongside Henry. He left his wife, Joan, literally holding the fort – in charge of a keep that was partially ruined and its outer ward indefensible. Along came storming troops of King Richard to lay siege to the castle. Lady Pelham, showing considerable gumption, rallied her garrison and pluckily held out against the royalist soldiers until relief arrived. Her spirited defence saved the day. And on Henry's accession to the throne, her husband received a grant of the castle.

The last reported sighting of the ghost of this doughty lady was in the 1970s, when she was seen on the walls of the keep. The name of Pelham has a strong link with Hastings, for some two hundred years after Lady Pelham's derring-do, Hastings Castle ruins also became the property of members of the Pelham family. It remained in the family's hands until 1951, when Hastings Corporation bought it from them (for £3,000).

Ghosts 2000

The Millennium Dome at Greenwich acquired its resident ghost at an early stage of development. In April 1998, reports emerged that the site of Britain's centrepiece for the Year 2000 celebrations had an unearthly intruder. The bearded ghost was seen in many parts of the site and, it was said, some people had reported hearing ghostly laughter.

The ghost was soon identified as being that of Sir George Livesey, former chairman of the old South Metropolitan Gas Company, which used to occupy the site. He was a popular man who did much good in the community. But apparently, having a statue of himself erected after his death in 1908 was not enough for Sir George, who stayed on in spirit to haunt the company which he had built up from 1881 into a well-established and respected firm. His ghost was much in evidence until the company closed down in 1971, as those who went to work there in its last years discovered.

Spectral Sir George caused havoc on numerous occasions. The offices were locked overnight, but when the staff came in next morning they would find the place in a real mess. A cleaner named Maisie Flegg, a spiritualist, made contact with the irascible ghost and found it to be none other than the former head of the company.

What with the demise of his beloved Gas Company

and the disturbance by the Dome builders, it was wondered, especially when things were not going too well on the site, whether ghostly Sir George was bent on showing his displeasure. Certainly, it seemed, he was going to be actively around for the year 2000 and after.

Perhaps future years will bring some answers about Sir George and his like, and the ghostly plane on which they exist, for it is depressing to think that we have landed men on the moon and sent probes to the other planets, yet still know so little about the mysterious world around and within ourselves.

Probably the most redundant question ever asked is, 'Do you believe in ghosts?' Anyone stoutly maintaining that there are no such things is like a soldier on the battlefield denying the existence of bullets when they are flying all around him.

A survey carried out for *The Sun* newspaper by MORI pollsters in 1998 found that more than nine out of ten people – ninety-two per cent of the population – believed in the paranormal. Two out of three believed in *déjà vu*, a feeling that they had done something or been somewhere before, while nearly half believed in the existence of ghosts, one in three of these having personally had a ghostly experience.

There is no denying that ghosts are around us all the time. They tend to appear unexpectedly, at any time of day or night and in any kind of earthly surrounding, and are most commonly seen not by professed ghosthunters, however well meaning these may be, but by ordinary people simply going about their everyday lives. They also seem to share many similar qualities of the 'other world', such as causing a remarkably sudden drop in temperature whenever they appear. So the real question still to be answered is, 'What are ghosts, and what causes them?' The twenty-first century may unravel these mysteries at last.

Meanwhile, a fire will be kept burning in an ancient inn in north Yorkshire, just in case – as insurance against any ghostly calamity happening there.

Local tradition says that disaster will strike the four hundred-year-old Saltersgate Inn, near Whitby, if the open fire ever goes out. In the past, when the flames threatened to die, pictures fell off the wall, appliances switched themselves off and on and the beer went flat. Some regulars would not come in if the fire was not roaring in its cast-iron range.

The tradition dates from 1796, when a customs officer was killed by smugglers and buried under the hearth. To avert suspicion, a fire was lit and kept burning. Should it ever go out, it was said, the murdered officer's spirit would be released to haunt the pub. So landlord Michael Milner, who took over the inn in the 1990s, continues to keep the fire burning winter and summer, all year long, even in a heatwave, for older customers told him that when the fire got very low strange things started happening, and he himself saw a picture above the fireplace jump off its big, strong hook for no reason.

So the fire at the Saltersgate Inn, which has been burning for two hundred years, will go on burning brightly, to the delight of visitors from many parts of this country and the world. And landlord Milner will be kept busy answering myriad questions, usually beginning with 'How do you clean your chimney?'

Even hauntings can be very basic.